J. L Jacobson

Poor Man's Gospel

J. L Jacobson

Poor Man's Gospel

ISBN/EAN: 9783743353787

Manufactured in Europe, USA, Canada, Australia, Japa

Cover: Foto ©Thomas Meinert / pixelio.de

Manufactured and distributed by brebook publishing software (www.brebook.com)

J. L Jacobson

Poor Man's Gospel

THE

POOR MAN'S GOSPEL.

COMPILED

FOR THE NEW WORLD.

[FROM THE FRENCH.]

BY

J. L. JACOBSON.

CHICAGO:
THE CHICAGO LEGAL NEWS CO.
1879.

Entered according to Act of Congress, in the year 1879, by
THE CHICAGO LEGAL NEWS COMPANY,
In the Office of the Librarian of Congress, at Washington.

STEREOTYPED, PRINTED, BOUND AND PUBLISHED, BY
THE CHICAGO LEGAL NEWS COMPANY.

PREFACE.

TO THE PEOPLE.

This book has been principally written for you; it is to you that I offer it. May it, in the midst of so many ills which fall to your lot, so many afflictions which weigh upon you, with little or no intermission, revive you and give you a little consolation!

To you who bear the burden of the day, may it be to your poor wearied spirit as is, in the corner of a field, at mid-day, the shade of a tree, howsoever insignificant, to him who has labored the whole morning under the burning rays of the sun.

You live in evil times, but those times will pass away.

After the rigors of winter, Providence brings back a season less harsh, and the little bird praises in its song the beneficent hand which has restored to it warmth and plenty, and its mate and its soft nest.

Hope and love. Hope sweetens all things, and love makes all things easy.

There are at this moment men who suffer much, because they have loved you much. I, their brother, I have written down the account of what they have done for you, and what has been done to them because of that; and when violence shall have expended its strength, I will publish it, and you will read it then with tears less bitter, and you will also love those men, who have loved you so well.

Now, if I should speak to you of their love and of their sufferings, I would be cast with them into the dungeon.

I would descend there with joy, if my going would lessen a little your wretchedness; but you would not thereby obtain any relief, and for that reason you must wait and pray God to shorten the trial.

Now it is man who judges and who punishes: soon it will be He who will judge. Happy those who shall see His justice!

I am old: listen to the words of an aged man.

The earth is dismal and dry, but she will become green again. The breath of the wicked will not eternally pass over her as a scorching wind.

What has been, Providence willed should be done for your instruction, that you may learn to be good and just, when your hour shall come.

When those who abuse their power shall have passed from before you as the mire from the gutter in a day of storm, then you will understand that the good alone is lasting, and you will fear to pollute the air, which the wind from heaven shall have made pure.

Prepare your souls for that time, for it is not far distant—it approaches.

Christ, nailed to the cross for you, has promised to deliver you.

Believe in His promise, and, to hasten its fulfilment, reform wherein you need reforming, practice all virtues, and love one another as the Savior of the human race has loved you, EVEN UNTO DEATH.

CONTENTS.

CHAPTER.		PAGE.
	Author's Preface	3
I.	The Light appears	11
II.	The Slaves of old and the Freemen of to-day	12
III.	The Rulers of this World	17
IV.	And they were sad	19
V.	One Father in Heaven and on Earth	22
VI.	Judge not	24
VII.	The Traveler and the Rock	25
VIII.	Labor enfranchised is Master of the World	28
IX.	Justice and Fraternity	30
X.	The Tramp in Jail	32
XI.	Union is Strength	35
XII.	The sacred War	38
XIII.	A sermon on Love	41
XIV.	The Proletarian	43
XV.	The Unbeliever	48

CONTENTS.

CHAPTER.		PAGE.
XVI.	The two Neighbors	50
XVII.	Prayer	53
XVIII.	The Reward of Justice and Fraternity	55
XIX.	Mother and Daughter	58
XX.	Society, its Past, Present and Future (Part I.)	61
XX.	Society, its Past, Present and Future (Part II.)	68
XX.	Society, its Past, Present and Future (Part III.)	72
XXI.	The City of Satan and the City of God	78
XXII.	The Seven Kings (Part I.)	81
XXII.	The Seven Kings (Part II.)	87
XXIII.	All are born equal	90
XXIV.	Dumb Animals and intelligent Animals	92
XXV.	Liberty	95
XXVI.	The Prayer of the Proletarians	97
XXVII.	Christ and the People	100
XXVIII.	Intolerance of Religion	103
XXIX.	The Law of Christ	106
XXX.	Father and Son	108
XXXI.	The Fruit of Sin	110
XXXII.	A Lesson from the Swallows	112
XXXIII.	Man, his Past, Present and Future	113
XXXIV.	The Reign of Satan	118
XXXV.	The War between Capital and Labor	120
XXXVI.	The second Coming of Christ	123
XXXVII.	The Mighty of Earth	126
XXXVIII.	The Persecution of Truth	127

CHAPTER.		PAGE.
XXXIX.	The Rights of the People and what has become of them	128
XL.	The Legacy to our Children	132
XLI.	Liberty and Justice	134
XLII.	The Slave and the Freeman	136
XLIII.	The two Idols	138
XLIV.	Nothing without God	141
XLV.	Observation of duty—the fulfilment of the Law	143
XLVI.	The Prophet	150
XLVII.	The Conspiracy of Evil	155
XLVIII.	The aged Man and the Pilgrim	161
XLIX.	The Millennium	171
L.	Life and Death	173
LI.	The true End of Life	175
LII.	We walk in Darkness	177
LIII.	The Church-yard	178
LIV.	The Exile	180
LV.	The Trinity	182
	The Dead	186

THE POOR MAN'S GOSPEL.

I.

THE LIGHT APPEARS.

In the Name of the Father, and of the Son, and of the Holy Ghost. Amen.

Glory to God in the highest, and on earth peace, good will toward men.

He that hath ears to hear, let him hear; he that hath eyes, let him open them and see, for the time approacheth.

The Father engendered His Son, His Promise, His Word, and the Word was made flesh, and dwelt among us; and He was in the world, and the world knew Him not.

The Son hath promised to send His Spirit of Comfort, the Holy Ghost, which proceedeth forth from the Father and from Him, and which is their mutual love; He shall come and renew the face of the earth, and it will be like a second creation.

Eighteen centuries ago, the Word strewed the seed Divine, and the Spirit of God fecundated it. Mankind have seen it in blossom, they have tasted of its fruit, of the fruit of the tree of life, transplanted to their wretched dwellings.

I say unto you, there was great joy among them when they saw the Light spring up, and when they felt themselves entirely penetrated with a celestial fire.

At present, the earth has become dark and cold again.

Our fathers have seen the sun decline. When it descended under the horizon, all humankind were startled. Then, there was in that night, I know not what, which is nameless. Children of the night! the Occident is dark, but in the Orient the light appears.

II.

THE SLAVES OF OLD AND THE FREEMEN OF TO-DAY.

In the beginning, it was not necessary for man to work in order to live: the earth spontaneously supplied all his wants.

But man did what was evil; and as he had revolted against God, the earth revolted against him.

That befell him, which befalls the son who revolts against his father: the father withdraws his love from him and abandons him to his fate; and the servants of the house refuse to attend upon him, and he goes away, looking here and there for his miserable livelihood, eating the bread which he has earned in the sweat of his face.

Ever since, then, God has condemned all men to work, and all have their labor, either of the body or of the mind; and those who say: I will not work! are the most wretched:

For, even as the worms devour a carcass, so the vices devour them, and if it is not vice, it is ennui.

And when the will of God was that man should work, He hid a treasure in labor, because He is a Father, and because the love of a Father never dies.

And for him who makes a good use of that treasure and does not squander it like a fool, there comes a time of rest, and then he is like man was in the beginning.

And God gave man this precept also: Help one another; for there are among you the strong and the weak, the infirm and the well; and yet all must live.

And if you act in this manner, all shall live, because I shall reward your compassion for your brother, and I shall render your sweat fertile.

And that which God has promised, always comes to pass, and never has he been seen in want of bread who helps his brother.

Now, in former times, there lived a wicked man, accursed of Heaven. And that man was strong, and hated work; so that he said to himself: What shall I do? If I do not work, I shall die, and work is intolerable to me.

Then a thought from Hell entered his head: During the night, he went and seized some of his brothers, whilst they were sleeping, and loaded them with chains.

For, he said to himself, I will compel them with rods and with lashes to work in my place, and I shall eat the fruit of their labor.

And he did what his brain had conceived, and others on seeing that did the same, and there were brothers no more: there were masters and slaves.

That day was a day of mourning over all the earth.

A long time afterwards there lived another man, more wicked than the first, and more accursed of Heaven.

Seeing that men had everywhere multiplied, and that their multitude was numberless, he said to himself:

I might perhaps succeed in binding some of them in chains, and in forcing them to work for me; but I should have to feed them, and that would diminish my gain. Let me do better: let them work for nothing! They shall die, it is true, but as their number is very great, I shall amass wealth before they shall have diminished much, and enough of them will always remain.

Now, all that multitude lived by what they received in exchange for their work.

Having spoken then in this manner, he addressed himself privately to a few of them, and said: You work during six hours, and are paid one piece of money for your labor: work during twelve hours, and you will earn two pieces of money, and live a great deal more comfortably, you, your wives and your children.

And they believed him.

After that, he said to them: You only work during half of the days of the year: work all the days of the year, and your earnings will be double.

And they believed him again.

Now it resulted therefrom that the quantity of labor having become one half greater, without the demand for labor increasing, the half of those who formerly lived by their labor, could find nowhere a person to employ them.

Then the wicked man, in whom they had believed, said to them: I will give work to all of you, upon condition that you shall not diminish your hours of labor, and that I shall pay you only the half of what you now receive: for I am willing to do you a service, but I cannot ruin myself for you.

And as they were starving, they, their wives and their children, they accepted the proposal of the wicked man, and they blessed him: for, said they, he gives us life anew.

And continuing to impose upon them in the same manner, the wicked man augmented their work ever more and more, and diminished their wages in the same proportion.

And they died from want, and others were eager to replace them: for indigence had become so general in that country, that whole families sold themselves for a piece of bread.

And the wicked man, who had told lies to his

brothers, amassed more wealth than the wicked man, who had bound them in chains.

The name of the latter is Tyrant; as for the other, he is unnamed out of Hell.

III.

THE RULERS OF THIS WORLD.

Why do the animals find their nourishment, each according to his kind ? It is because no one among them takes away that of the others, and because each contents himself with that which supplies his needs.

If in a hive, one bee should say : All the honey which is here, is mine, and thereupon should dispose of the fruits of the common labor as it pleased, what would become of the other bees ?

The earth is like a great hive, and men are the bees.

Each bee has a right to the portion of honey, necessary to its subsistence, and if, among men, there be any who are in want of that portion, it is because justice and fraternity have disappeared from among them.

Justice—that is life ; and fraternity—that is life also, and a more sweet and fruitful life.

There have arisen false prophets, who have persuaded some men that all others were born for them; and what these have believed, others have believed also on the word of the false prophets.

When this false teaching prevailed, the angels in heaven wept, for they foresaw that much violence, and many crimes, and many evils would spread abroad over the earth.

Men, equal among themselves, are born for God alone, and whoever says the contrary, utters a blasphemy.

Whosoever will be great among you, shall be your minister; and whosoever of you will be the chiefest, shall be servant of all.

The law of God is a law of love, and love does not exalt itself over others, but it sacrifices itself to others.

He who says within his heart: I am not as other men, but all others have been given to me, that I may command them, and dispose of them and what is theirs according to my fancy: that man is the child of Satan.

And Satan is the king of this world, for he is the king of all those who think and act after this manner; and those who think and act thus, have made themselves, by his counsels, masters of the world.

But their empire will be only for a time, and we approach the end of that time.

A great battle will be fought, and the angel of justice and the angel of love will fight with those who have taken arms to re-establish among men the reign of justice and the reign of love.

And many will perish in that combat, and their names will remain on earth as rays from God's glory.

Therefore, ye who suffer, take courage, strengthen your hearts : for to-morrow will be the day of trial, the day when each must surrender, with joy, his life for his brothers ; and the day that will follow, will be the day of deliverance.

IV.

AND THEY WERE SAD.

The sun had risen in his splendor; his light streamed over the declivities of the mountains, pierced through the dark shadows of the forest, and sparkled in the dew, covering the light gossamers, which like an impalpable, movable net-work were spread over the meadows and fields; fresh odors—like unto the breath of the genii of the earth—perfumed the calm air; mysterious voices, heard from afar, murmured unknown sounds, scarcely perceptible to the ear: the last echo of the dreams of night.

Great art Thou, oh God! Thou art great in Thy works.

And I saw come forth from the huts, scattered here and there over the hills and in the valleys, old men and young men, all of them pale, emaciated, and bent under the burden of agricultural implements. They walked slowly, as if, in addition, they were bearing along with them I know not what internal load. Now and then, halting, their eyes dwelt in thought upon all these divine splendors.

And they were sad.

The trees, full of sap, said to them: Behold these blossoms; they will soon turn into fruit, which will ripen for you.

And they were sad.

The vine spoke to them: In my branches I prepare in secret a juice, which will infuse new life into you, and warm your frozen limbs, when winter shall have come.

And they were sad.

The meadows spoke: We have prepared a banquet for your sheep, your oxen and your cows;

bring them here, and in a hundred various ways, they will repay to you, what we shall give them.

And they were sad.

And the fields also spoke to them: Are your barns ready? All the day and the night, we are working in order to fill them. Therefore, take ye no thought neither for yourselves, nor for your wives, nor for your little children. God has bidden us to provide abundantly for their wants.

And they were sad.

All Nature cried aloud to them:

I am your Mother; come here, my children! all of ye, come and drink plentifully at my inexhaustible breast!

And they were sad, and their chests heaved, and great tears trickled from their eyes.

What does that signify, oh God? and what secret sorrow lies hidden, then, at the bottom of man's heart?

They are sad, because those fruits will not ripen for them; because the juice of the vine shall not warm them in winter; because they shall have no share, neither in the wool of their sheep, nor in the milk of their cows, nor in the flesh of their oxen; because others shall cut the grain from their fields, and reap where they have sown in fatigue and in the sweat of their face; because they already hear their little children cry with hunger; and because they see the hearts of those who gave them life breaking; because a violent race, devoid of pity and love, has placed itself between them and the common Mother; and because that race will not tolerate their lips at her inexhaustible breast!

And Thy justice, oh God?

My day of justice will come, doubt it not; and that day will be a holy day in Heaven, and a day of great joy on earth!

V.

ONE FATHER IN HEAVEN AND ON EARTH.

You are all children of the same father, and the same mother has nursed you; why then do you not love one another as brothers? and why do you treat one another rather as enemies?

He who loves not his brother, is seven times accursed, and he who makes himself the enemy of his brother, is accursed seventy times seven.

This is why kings and princes, and all those whom the world calls great, have been accursed:

they have not loved their brothers, and they have treated them as enemies.

Love one another, and you will fear neither the great, nor princes, nor kings.

They are strong against you, only because you are not united, only because you do not love one another as brothers.

Say not: He is of one nation, and I am of another nation. For all nations on earth had the same father, who is Adam, and they have the same Father in Heaven, who is God.

If one member is injured, the whole body suffers. You are all of the same body: one of you cannot be oppressed, without all being oppressed.

If a wolf springs upon a flock, he does not devour the whole flock immediately: he seizes one sheep and eats it. Then, his hunger having returned, he seizes another and eats it, and so continues until the last, for his hunger always comes back.

Be not as the sheep, who when the wolf has carried away one of them, are frightened for a moment, and then begin to graze again. For, think they, perhaps he will content himself with a first or a second victim: and wherefore should I be uneasy about those whom he devours? What does that matter to me? it will only leave so much the more grass for me.

Verily, I say unto you: Those who think in this way, are marked to be the food of the beast which lives on flesh and blood.

VI.

JUDGE NOT

When you see a man, led to prison or to the scaffold, do not cry out immediately: He is a wicked man, who has committed a crime against his fellow-men.

For it may be that he is a good man, who wished to serve his fellow-men, and who is punished therefor by their oppressors.

When you see a whole nation, loaded with chains and given up to the executioner, do not cry out immediately: That nation is a violent nation, which disturbed the peace of the earth.

For it may be that it is a nation of martyrs, which dies for the welfare of mankind.

Eighteen centuries ago, in a city of the Orient, the pontiffs and the kings of that time, nailed to a cross, after having scourged him, a rebel, a blasphemer, as they called him.

The day of his death, there was great terror in Hell, and great joy in Heaven.

For the blood of the Just One had saved the world.

VII.

THE TRAVELER AND THE ROCK.

When a tree stands alone, it is shaken by the winds and stripped of its leaves; and its branches, instead of rising, droop as if they were seeking the earth.

When a plant grows alone, finding no shelter against the burning heat of the sun, it fades away, withers, and dies.

When man is alone, the breath of power bears him downward to the earth, and the scorching covetousness of the great of this world absorbs the sap which should nourish him.

Be not then as the plant and the tree which grow solitary: but be united the one with the other, and mutually lean on, and shelter one another.

As long as you shall be disunited, and every one shall think of himself alone, you have nothing to expect but suffering, and affliction, and oppression.

What is feebler than the sparrow, and more defenseless than the swallow? Nevertheless, when the bird of prey appears, the swallows and the sparrows succeed in driving him away, by gathering around, and pursuing him in a body.

Take example from the sparrow and the swallow.

He who separates himself from his brothers, fear follows him wherever he goes, sits down by him when he takes rest, and does not leave him during his sleep.

Therefore, if you are asked: How many are you? answer: We are one, for our brothers, are ourselves, and we, are our brothers.

God has made neither small nor great, neither masters nor slaves, neither kings nor subjects: He has made all men equal.

But among men, some have more power either of body, of mind, or of will, and those are the ones who seek to subject others, when pride or covetousness extinguishes in them the love for their brothers.

And God knew that it would be so, and therefore He has commanded men to love one another, so that they might be united, and the weak not fall under the oppression of the strong.

For he who is stronger than one, will be less strong than two; and he who is stronger than two, will be less strong than four; and therefore the weak will fear nothing, when, loving one another, they shall be truly united.

A man traveled in the mountains, and he arrived in a place, where a huge rock, having rolled down on the path, filled it up entirely, and except the path, there was no other passage, neither on the left, nor on the right.

Now, that man, seeing that he could not continue his journey, on account of the rock, endeavored to remove it, to make himself a passage, and he wearied himself very much in the attempt, and all his efforts were vain.

Seeing which, he sat down, filled with sadness, and said: What will become of me, when night comes on, and overtakes me in this solitude, without food, without shelter, without any defense, at the hour when the wild beasts come out to search for their prey?

And while he was absorbed in that thought, it chanced that another traveler came, and the latter, having attempted to do what the first had attempted, and having also found himself unable to remove the rock, sat down in silence and bowed his head.

And after this one, several others came, and not

one was able to remove the rock, and the fear of all was great.

Finally one of them said to the others: Brothers, let us pray to our Father who is in Heaven: perhaps He may take pity on us in our distress.

And this counsel was heeded, and they prayed from their heart to the Father who is in Heaven.

And when they had prayed, he who had said: Let us pray, spoke again: Brothers, that which no one of us has been able to do alone, who knows, but we may accomplish it together?

And they rose up, and all together they pushed against the rock, and the rock yielded, and they proceeded on their way in peace.

The traveler is man, the journey is life, the rock is the trouble which he meets at every step on his path.

No man would be able to raise that rock alone; but God has measured the weight of it, so that it never blocks the way of those who journey together.

VIII.

LABOR ENFRANCHISED IS MASTER OF THE WORLD.

You are in this world like strangers.

Go North and South, to the Orient and to the

Occident, in whatever place you shall come, you will find a man, who will drive you away, saying: That piece of ground is mine.

And after having traveled over all countries, you will return, convinced that there is nowhere a poor little corner of earth, where your wife in travail may bear her firstborn; where you may take rest in old age, your labor finished; where, after your death, your children may inter your bones as in a place of your own.

That is, indeed, very sad.

And, yet, you must not grieve too much, for it is written of Him, who saved the human race:

The fox has his hole, and the bird of the air has its nest; but the Son of man hath not where to lay His head.

Now, he became poor, in order to teach you to endure poverty.

It is not that poverty comes from God, but it is a consequence of the corruption and of the wicked lusts of men, and this is why there will always be the poor.

Poverty is the child of sin, the germ of which is in each man, and of servitude, the germ of which is in every society.

There will always be poor, because man never can destroy the sin within himself.

There will always be fewer poor, because gradually servitude will disappear from society.

Do you wish to labor for the destruction of poverty, work at the destruction of sin, first in yourselves, then in others, and of servitude in society.

It is not by taking away what belongs to others, that you can destroy poverty; for how, in creating the poor, would one diminish the number of the poor?

Every one has a right to preserve what he has, except for that, no one would possess anything.

But each has a right to acquire by his labor what he has not, except for that, poverty would be eternal.

Enfranchise therefore your labor, enfranchise your arms, and poverty shall be among men only as an exception, which God suffers in order to remind them of the infirmity of their nature, and the mutual assistance and love which they owe the one to the other.

IX.

JUSTICE AND FRATERNITY.

When the whole earth groaned in the expectation of deliverance, a voice arose from Judea, the voice of Him who came to suffer and to die for His brothers, and whom some called in scorn the Son of the carpenter.

The Son of the carpenter, then, poor and forlorn in this world, said:

Come unto me, all ye that labor, and are heavy laden, and I will give you rest.

And from that day to the present time, not one of those who have believed in Him, has remained without relief in his misery.

To cure the evils which afflict mankind, He preached to all justice, which is the commencement of fraternity, and fraternity which is the consummation of justice.

Now, justice commands us to respect the right of others, and sometimes fraternity bids us give up our own right, for the sake of peace or some other blessing.

What would be the world, if right ceased to reign, if each were not secure in his person, and could not enjoy without fear that which belongs to him?

Better to live in the midst of the forests, than in a society, thus given up to plunder.

What you shall lay hold of to-day, another will

snatch from you to-morrow. Men will be more wretched than the birds of the air, from whom the other birds ravish neither food nor nest.

What is a poor man? A man who as yet has no property.

What does he wish for? To cease to be poor, that is to say: to acquire property.

Now, he who robs, who plunders, what does he do but to abolish, so far as is in his power, the very right of property?

To plunder, to steal then, is to attack the poor man as well as the rich man; it is to overthrow the foundation of all society among men.

Whoever has nothing, would be unable to acquire property, except that others already have property; because they alone can give him something in exchange for his labor.

Order is the advantage, the interest of all.

Drink not at the cup of crime: at the bottom is bitter sorrow, and anguish, and death.

X.

THE TRAMP IN JAIL.

Oh! who shall give back to me the valley where

I was born; and my rocks; and the high pine-trees, sown over their declivities; and the verdant meadows, where—in limpid water, hidden under the flowery grass—I bathed my feet at the melting of the snow?

Between the earth and me, poor child of the mountains, they have placed a massive wall and iron bars.

When I appeared before them, they asked me: How do you live?

By the work of my hands, I answered, but all at present refuse it, and nothing remains for me to do, but to starve and die.

You die with hunger? 'tIs crime! And your dwelling-place? Have you a dwelling-place?

The night having come, and all the doors being shut to me for want of money, I seek shelter where Providence guides me.

You have no dwelling-place? 'tIs crime! Law is express on that point: Prison!

Impostors, who call yourselves the disciples of the Son of Man, of Him who went through this world, poor and forlorn, and had not where to lay His head, look up to His image above you, behold the indignant expression of His face, and see His lips open in saint-like wrath to accurse both you and your laws!

Are not the air and the sun the property of all? Has God constructed jails for any of His creatures?

Sheperds of my native valley, rejoice in your humble huts! There, at least, poverty is no crime, and there the traveler always finds a little milk and a crust of bread to appease his hunger, and dried leaves to rest on.

In the midst of you, my brothers! how happily passed the blessed days of my youth! How deliciously my thoughts would wander in the boundless realms of fancy, while reclining on the greensward, at the foot of a moss-grown rock, I inhaled the intoxicating fragrance of our perfumed plants, listening to the sweet song of the thrush, and the roar of the torrent, which rolled on and dashed its spray on the pebbles at the bottom of the ravine!

How thickly these reminiscences crowd upon me! I see the light clouds creeping up the mountain-ridges, folding and folding again into a thousand fantastic shapes, then rising toward their top, and surrounding them with a dark diadem.

What is the meaning of that scarcely perceptible point above me? It is the eagle, who pursues his calm, majestic flight through immensity. He, the eagle, is free!

And the wild goat also is free on its solitary rock, and the bear is free in its cavern, and the bird in the woods, and the insect in the grass.

Oh! wherefore cannot I be the insect in the grass, the bird in the woods, the bear in its cavern, or the wild goat on its solitary rock!

All creatures go and come as they please, and breathe, under God's heaven, an air which none metes out to them.

The pauper is the only exception; the pauper is an outlaw; he is the outcast of creation.

Who could have foretold, oh God! that the day would come, when I should lament my being a man!

XI.

UNION IS STRENGTH.

When one of you suffers an injustice, when, on his way through the world, the oppressor overthrows and places his foot upon him; if he complains, no one hears him.

The cry of the poor ascends to God, but reaches not the ear of man.

And I asked myself: Whence comes this evil? Can it have been the will of Him who created the poor as well as the rich, the weak as well as the strong, to take away from the one all fear in his iniquity, from the other all hope in his wretchedness?

And I perceived that this was a horrible thought, a blasphemy against God.

Because each of you loves only himself, because he separates himself from his brothers, because he is alone and wishes to be alone, his complaint is not heard.

In spring, when everything revives, there comes from the grass a noise which arises like a long murmur.

That noise, formed by so many noises, that one would not be able to count them, is the voice of an innumerable number of poor, little, invisible creatures.

Alone, no one of them would be heard: all together, they make themselves heard.

You also are hidden in the grass; why does no voice come forth from you?

When one desires to cross a rapid river, a long line is made in two rows, and thus clinging together, those who, alone, would not have been able to resist the force of the waters, pass over without trouble.

Act in this manner, and you will break the current of iniquity, which sweeps you away when you are alone, and casts you bruised upon the bank.

Let your resolutions be slow, but firm. Yield not to a first, nor to a second impulse.

But if some injustice has been done to you, commence by banishing from your heart every feeling of hatred, and then, raising your hands and eyes on high, say to your Father, who is in Heaven:

Oh, Father! Thou art the protector of the innocent and of the oppressed; for it is Thy love which has created the world, and it is Thy justice which governs it.

Thy will is that it reign on earth, and the wicked oppose their evil wish to it.

For this reason, we have resolved to fight against the wicked.

Oh, Father! give wisdom to our spirit, and strength to our arms!

When you shall have prayed thus from the bottom of your soul, battle and fear nothing.

If, at first, victory seems to elude you, it is but a trial, it will return again: for your blood will be like the blood of Abel, killed by Cain, and your death will be like the death of martyrs.

XII.

THE SACRED WAR.

Young soldier, whither dost thou go?

I go to battle for God and the altars of my native land.

May thine arms be blessed, young soldier!

Young soldier, whither dost thou go?

I go to battle for justice, for the holy cause of the people, for the sacred rights of mankind.

May thine arms be blessed, young soldier!

Young soldier, whither dost thou go?

I go to battle for the deliverance of my brothers from oppression, to break their chains and the chains of the world.

May thine arms be blessed, young soldier!

Young soldier, whither dost thou go?

I go to battle against the men of iniquity, in favor of those whom they crush and trample under their feet, against the master for the slave, against the tyrant for liberty.

May thine arms be blessed, young soldier!

Young soldier, whither dost thou go?

I go to battle that all may no longer be the spoil of the few, to raise up the drooping heads, and to support the knees which bend.

May thine arms be blessed, young soldier!

Young soldier, whither dost thou go?

I go to battle that the fathers may no longer curse the day, on which was said to them: A son is born unto you; nor the mothers that on which they pressed him for the first time to their breast.

May thine arms be blessed, young soldier!

Young soldier, whither dost thou go?

I go to battle that the brother may no longer be afflicted at seeing his sister fade away like the plant which the earth refuses to nourish; that the sister may no longer gaze in tears upon her brother who parts, and shall return no more.

May thine arms be blessed, young soldier!

Young soldier, whither dost thou go?

I go to battle that each may eat in peace the fruit of his toil; to dry the tears of the little children who ask for bread, and receive the answer: There is no more bread: what remained has been taken away from us.

May thine arms be blessed, young soldier!

Young soldier, whither dost thou go?

I go to battle for the poor, that he may not always be despoiled of his share in the common heritage.

May thine arms be blessed, young soldier!

Young soldier, whither dost thou go?

I go to battle and to drive hunger from the huts, to bring back to homes abundance, security and gladness.

May thine arms be blessed, young soldier!

Young soldier, whither dost thou go?

I go to battle to restore to those whom their oppressors have cast into the depths of dungeons, the air which their lungs need and the light which their eyes seek.

May thine arms be blessed, young soldier!

Young soldier, whither dost thou go?

I go to battle to overturn the barriers which separate nations, and prevent them from embracing as sons of the same father, created to live united in the same love.

May thine arms be blessed, young soldier!

Young soldier, whither dost thou go?

I go to battle to liberate thought, speech, conscience, from the tyranny of man.

May thine arms be blessed, young soldier!

Young soldier, whither dost thou go?

I go to battle for the eternal laws, descended from on high, for justice which protects right, for fraternity which mitigates the evils which are inevitable.

May thine arms be blessed, young soldier!

Young soldier, whither dost thou go?

I go to battle that all may have in heaven a God, and on earth a fatherland.

May thine arms be blessed, seven times blessed, young soldier!

XIII.

A SERMON ON LOVE.

You have only a day to spend here on earth; act in such a manner that you may spend it in peace.

Peace is the fruit of love; for in order to live in peace, we must bear with a great many things.

None is perfect, each has his failings; each hangs upon the other, and love alone renders that weight light.

If you cannot bear with your brother, how will your brother with you?

It is written of the son of Mary: that having loved His own which were in the world, He loved them unto the end.

For that reason: love your brother who is in the world, and love him unto the end.

Love is indefatigable, it never grows weary. Love is inexhaustible; it lives and is born anew in the living, and the more it pours out, the fuller its fountain.

Whosoever loves himself better than he loves his brother, is not worthy of Christ: who *died* for His brothers. Have you given away every thing you possess? go and give up your life also: love will restore all to you.

Verily, I say unto you: the heart of the man that loves, is a paradise on earth. He has God within him, for God is love.

The wicked man loves not, he covets: he hungers and thirsts for everything; his eye, like unto the eye of the serpent, fascinates and allures, but only to devour.

Love rests at the bottom of every pure soul, like a drop of dew in the calyx of a flower.

Oh! if you knew what it is to love!

You say that you love: and many of your brothers are in want of bread to sustain their life; in want of clothing to cover their naked limbs; in want of a roof to shelter themselves; in want of a handful of straw to sleep on—whilst you have all things in abundance.

You say that you love: and a great number there are who, destitute of succor, pine away their lives in sickness on a miserable couch—poor wretches who weep, whilst no one weeps with them; how many little children there are who, shivering with cold, go from door to door, begging the rich for the crumbs from their table, and do not obtain them.

You say that you love your brothers:—and what then would you do, if you *hated* them?

Verily, verily, I say unto you: whosoever, being able to do so, does not relieve his brother who suffers—is an Enemy to his brother; and whosoever, being able to do so, does not give nourishment to his starving brother—is the Murderer of his brother.

XIV.

THE PROLETARIAN.*

Take pity, oh God, on the poor proletarian!
When I came into this world, my father was no

---

*Proletarian: A man who has no property, and depends entirely on his physical strength for support.

more. One day, the fleshless spectre, called Misery, entered his dwelling; he struggled against it hand to hand; he struggled for a long time; but finally his strength abandoned him. Then came down the angel who delivers, and inclining over his couch: Thou hast, said the angel, accomplished thy rough task in this world; now, pass on to a better life.

My mother, with her own hands, dressed him for the grave; then she remained alone. Alone? No; the spectre was constantly there.

When the time of her delivery had come, she gave birth to me, with great pains, and she cried. She cried, my mother, for she had no swaddling-clothes to wrap her first-born in.

And later, her tears fell more abundantly still, when she saw that her milk was drying up for want of food, and that the heat of her breast, as little as her feeble breath, were able to warm the emaciated limbs of her child.

By strength of love, making a sacrifice of her own life, she preserved mine. Working all the day, all the night long, without fire during the winter, and exposed to the burning heat in summer, her only care, during all those long and wearisome hours, consisted in protecting me from the sufferings she endured for my sake, and her only delight was to smile on me.

However, I grew up. She redoubled her efforts, in order that a little instruction might smooth the path, which I was to tread in later years. Oh! how her heart leaped with joy, when the school was over, on seeing her child return gay and contented —as we are at that age—dressed in his little blouse, with a leathern belt, girded round his waist, a cap on his golden locks, and the strap, which contained his books, dangling from his shoulder!

Then came the time of my apprenticeship. I rejoiced at the idea that the time would not be long, before I should be able to pay back to her, from whom I had received everything, a little of that which her inexhaustible tenderness had bestowed upon me. In my dreams, I saw myself bringing her the fruit of my first labor, and saying to her: Now, let the toil be mine, mother! and do you take repose.

Alas! in a few years she had worn out her whole existence. He who from Heaven had made himself the support, the comforter of the poor widow, called her back to Him. Her decline was rapid. At last, she expired in my arms. The very moment she breathed her last, her mute lips were smiling at me, and her dying look blessed me for a last time.

When they lowered her into the grave, and the sound of the falling mould grew duller and more dull, Thou alone, oh God! Thou knowest what passed within me.

Henceforth, standing alone in this world, I lived as if I did not belong to it, feeding on reminiscences, vague reveries and melancholy hopes.

One day, in the midst of those sombre shadows, a gentler light appeared to me. On my solitary path, Providence guided a youthful maiden, an orphan like myself. The dew of spring is less pure, than was her heart. After a first glance, our eyes looked downward, and it was our silence alone which spoke. Our souls, inclining the one toward the other, in that moment were united forever.

No! heaven, among its purest ecstacies, has nothing that can be compared to the ravishing hours which flew away during our conversations. I said to her: There is not one who cares either for you or for me; to us two the world is a wilderness. My poor, little turtle-dove of the forest, I will go and look for your food, and I will build you a nest, where you shall repose, sheltered from cold and storm.

Whereto she answered: And whilst I shall be occupied with other cares during your absence, at your return my caresses will soothe away your weariness: but, oh my well-beloved! come back quickly!

I wasted away in the longing for her possession; but she, wiser than I was, repressed my ardor, and said: Think of those who will come; let us first save a little.

The term of this long waiting was nearly ended, when, of a sudden: *Labor is no longer in demand.* They cut down the wages, and they go on cutting them down: take that, or starve!

Our laboring strength is all that we possess; other property than our muscles we have not! That is the way in which the proletarians make answer. And they concert together that they may live: they are thrown into prison.

Oh, justice of mankind! how shalt thou tremble in thy fear that day, when thou art judged by the Justice of God!

The rest is but one lugubrious dream.

During the long and dreary weeks of my confinement, I saw her twice, thrice perhaps, through the grates of my cell. The last time, her sunken eyes sparkled with strange fire, her knees were bent, she could scarcely stand.

Thereafter, I did not see her again.

Oh, mother darling! Oh, my dearest beloved! Is it you whom I perceive there above me in that light? Who calls me? Is it you? Do not forsake me! oh, do not forsake me! I feel my chains give way: one moment, one single moment more, and we shall be reunited.

Take pity, oh God, on the poor proletarian!

XV.

THE UNBELIEVER.

You will meet men, who love not God, and who fear Him not: shun them, for a vapor of execration issues from them.

Shun the impious, for his breath kills; but hate him not, for who knows, if God has not already changed his heart?

The man who, even sincerely, says: I believe not, often deceives himself. Deep down in the soul, at the very bottom, there is a root of faith, which withers not.

The word which denies God, scorches the lips over which it passes, and the mouth which opens to blaspheme, is a vent of hell.

The impious is alone in the Universe. All creatures praise God, all that feel bless Him, all that think adore: the sun by day and stars by night sing Him in their mysterious language.

He has written on the firmament His name thrice holy.

Glory to God in the highest!

He has written it likewise in the heart of man, and the good man preserves it there with love; but others endeavor to blot it out.

Peace on earth to men of good will!

Their sleep is sweet, and their death is still more sweet, for they know that they return to their Father.

Even as the poor laborer, at the decline of day, quits the fields, seeks his hut, and sitting down at the door, forgets his weariness, in viewing the heavens: so, when evening comes, the man of hope returns with joy to his Father's house, and, sitting on the threshold, forgets the toils of the exile in the visions of eternity.

XVI.

THE TWO NEIGHBORS.

Two men were neighbors, and each of them had a wife and several small children, and his sole labor was to make for them a living.

And one of these two men made himself very uneasy, saying: If I die, or if I fall sick, what will become of my wife and my children?

And this thought did not quit him, and it gnawed at his heart, as a worm gnaws the fruit, in which it is hidden.

Now, although the same thought had come likewise to the other father, he would not entertain it; for, said he, God, who knows all His creatures, and who watches over them, will also watch over me, and over my wife, and over my children.

And this one lived tranquilly, whereas the first did not taste a moment of peace, nor of mental enjoyment.

One day, as he was laboring in the fields, sad and downcast because of his fear, he saw a number of birds enter a bush, come out, and soon return to it again.

And having approached, he saw two nests placed side by side, and in each several young birds newly hatched and still featherless.

And when he had returned to his labor, from time to time he raised his eyes and watched the birds, how they went and came, carrying food to their young.

But, behold! at the moment that one of the mothers came back with food in her bill, a vulture seizes her, bears her away, and the poor mother, vainly struggling in its talon, uttered piercing cries.

At this sight, the man who labored felt his soul more troubled than before: for, thought he, the death of the mother is the death of the children. Mine have also but me. What will become of them, if I die?

And the whole day he was gloomy and sad, and at night he slept not.

The next morning, on returning to the fields, he said to himself: I will go and see the young of that poor mother: several of them, without doubt, have already perished. And he turned his steps toward the bush.

And looking, he saw the young in good health; not one of them seemed to have suffered.

And surprised at this, he hid himself to watch what would take place.

And after a short time, he heard a feeble cry, and he saw the second mother, bringing in haste the food which she had gathered, and she distributed it to all the young, without distinction, and there was enough for all, and the orphans were not forsaken in their distress.

And the father, who had doubted Providence, related, in the evening, to the other father what he had seen.

And this one said to him: Wherefore be uneasy? God never abandons His own. His love has secrets which we know not. Let us believe, let us hope, let us love, and pursue our path in peace.

If I die before you, you will be a father to my children; if you die before me, I will be the father of yours.

And if we both die, before they are old enough to provide for themselves, they shall have for a father the Father who is in Heaven.

XVII.

PRAYER.

When you have prayed, do you not feel your heart lighter, and your soul more content?

Prayer makes affliction less grievous, and joy more pure: it imparts to the one I know not what of strength and of sweetness, and to the other a celestial perfume.

What do ye on the earth, and have ye nothing to ask of Him who placed you here?

You are a traveler in search of his fatherland. Walk not with head bent down: you must raise your eyes to know your way.

Your fatherland is heaven; and when you look up to heaven, does it move you in no way? does no desire press upon you? or is that desire dumb?

There are some who say: Of what benefit is prayer? God is too far above us to listen to creatures so pitiful.

And who then made these pitiful creatures, who gave them feeling, thought and speech, if not God?

And if He has been so good to them, was it to cast them off afterwards, and to keep them afar from Him?

Verily, I say unto you, whosoever says within his heart, that God despises His works, blasphemes against God.

There are others who say: What is the use of praying? Does God not know better than we, what we need?

God does know better than you, what you need, and it is for this reason, that He wishes you to ask it of Him; for God Himself is your first need, and to pray to God, is commencing to possess God.

The father knows the needs of his son; must that be a reason, why the son never should have a word of prayer and of thanksgiving for his father?

When the animals suffer, when they are in fear, or when they are hungry, they utter plaintive cries. These cries are the prayer which they address to God, and God listens. Should man be then, in creation, the only being whose voice never ascends to the ear of the Creator?

Sometimes there passes over the fields a wind which dries up the plants, and then their withered stems are seen to droop to the earth; but, moistened by the dew, they regain their freshness, and raise anew their languishing heads.

There are always blasting winds, which pass over

the soul of man, and dry it up. Prayer is the dew which revives it.

XVIII.

THE REWARD OF JUSTICE AND FRATERNITY.

Not to do unto others, what we should not wish that others should do unto us, that is justice.

To do unto others, on every occasion, what we should wish that others should do unto us, that is fraternity.

A man lived by his labor, he, his wife and his little children; and as he enjoyed good health, had vigorous arms, and easily found employment, he could, without much difficulty, provide for his subsistence and that of his family.

But it came to pass that times having become very hard over all the country, labor was in little demand, because it no longer yielded profit to employers, and at the same time the price of the necessaries of life advanced.

The man of labor and his family, then, began to suffer much. Having soon exhausted his small savings, he was forced to sell, piece by piece, first his furniture, then most of his clothing; and when he had thus stripped himself, he remained, deprived of all resources, face to face with hunger. And hunger alone had not entered his dwelling: sickness had come in with it.

Now, this man had two neighbors, the one more rich, the other less.

He called upon the first, and said: We are in want of everything, I, my wife and my children: have compassion on us.

The rich man answered him: How can I help that? When you have worked for me, have I ever withheld your wages, or have I ever deferred the payment of them? I never did any wrong, neither to you, nor to any other: my hands are clean of all iniquity. I feel sorrow for your distress, but every one must think of himself in these bad times: who knows how long they may last?

The poor father answered not, and slowly returning home, his heart full of anguish, he met his other neighbor, who was less rich.

The latter, seeing him pensive and sad, said to him: What troubles you? there is care on your brow and tears in your eyes?

And the father, with a trembling voice, made known his distress to him.

When he had finished: Wherefore, said the

other to him, be so despondent? Are we not brothers! And how could I abandon my brother in his troubles? Come with me, and we will share that which I enjoy through the goodness of God.

In this manner, the family which suffered was relieved, until they could provide for themselves.

Several years passed by. The two rich neighbors appeared before the Sovereign Judge of human actions.

And the Judge said to the first: My eye has followed thee on earth: thou hast refrained from wronging thy fellow-men, from violating their rights; thou hast rigorously accomplished the strict law of justice; but in that accomplishment, thou hast lived for thyself alone; thy hard, unfeeling soul has not understood the law of love. And now, in this new world, where thou enterest poor and naked, unto thee shall be done as thou didst unto others. Thou hast kept for thyself alone the blessings which fell to thy lot; thou hast bestowed nothing upon thy brothers: nothing shall be given to thee. Thou hast thought of thyself alone: go now, and live on thyself.

And turning towards the second, the Judge said to him: Forasmuch as thou hast not only been just, but as fraternity has penetrated thy heart; because that thy hand opened itself to distribute among thy brothers, who were less happy, the blessings of which thou wast the depositary; and since thy hand wiped away the tears of those who wept: greater blessings shall be given unto thee. Go and receive the reward of him who has fully accomplished his duties: the law of justice and the law of love.

XIX.

MOTHER AND DAUGHTER.

It was a winter-night. The wind howled without, and the snow whitened the roofs.

Beneath one of those roofs, in a narrow chamber, were sitting, at their needle-work, a woman with white hair and a young maiden.

And from time to time, the aged woman warmed at a small brasier her thin hands. A lamp of clay shed its feeble light around in this wretched abode, and a ray from the lamp seemed to expire upon a picture of the Blessed Virgin, hanging on the wall.

And the young maiden, lifting her eyes, gazed in silence, for a few moments, upon the white-haired woman; then said to her: Mother, you have not always been in such poverty.

And there was in her voice a sweetness and a tenderness indescribable.

And the white-haired woman replied: My daughter, God is our Master: His doing is well done.

Having uttered these words, she was silent for a time; then she resumed:

When I lost your father, it was an affliction which I believed beyond consolation: however, you were left to me; but I thought at that time of only one thing.

Later, I knew that if he had lived, and had seen us in such distress, his heart would have broken; and I have realized that God had been good to him.

The young maiden made no answer, but dropped her head, and a few tears, which she strove to hide, fell upon the linen which she held in her hands.

The mother went on: God, who has been good to him, has also been good to us. Of what have we been in want, while so many others are in want of everything?

It is true, we have been compelled to accustom ourselves to a little, and to earn that little by our labor, but does that little not suffice us? and have not all, from the beginning, been condemned to live by their labor?

God, in His kindness, has given us every day our daily bread: and how many have it not? a shelter—and how many know not where to retire?

He has given you, my daughter, to me: of what should I complain?

At these last words, the young maiden, much moved, sunk down at her mother's knee, took her hands, kissed them, and lying upon her bosom, wept.

And the mother, making an effort to raise her voice, said: My daughter, happiness is not possessing much, but hoping and loving much.

Our hope is not of this world, nor is our love, and if it be, it is only fleeting.

After God, you are my all in this world; but this world passes away like a dream, and this is why my love rises with you to another world.

When I carried you unborn, one day I prayed more ardently the Virgin Mary, and she appeared to me during my sleep, and with a celestial smile, she seemed to present to me a little child.

And I took the infant which she offered me, and as I held it in my arms, the Virgin-Mother placed on its head a crown of white roses.

A few months later, you were born, and the sweet vision was always before my eyes.

Saying this, the white-haired woman trembled, and pressed to her heart the young maiden.

A short time after that, a devout soul saw two shining forms ascend toward Heaven, and a group of angels bore them company, and the air resounded with their songs of gladness.

XX.

SOCIETY, ITS PAST, PRESENT AND FUTURE.

PART I.

ALL things in this world are not like they ought to be. There are too many evils, and those evils are too great. Such can never have been the will of God.

All men, born from one and the same father, should have formed one single, great family, united by the sweet tie of fraternal love. That family, in its growth, would have resembled a tree, the trunk of which, on shooting up, produces numerous branches, whence spring boughs and twigs, and from these, others still; all of them nourished by the same sap, all animated by the same life.

In a household, all have in view the benefit of all, because all love one another, and because all have a share in the common weal. There is not one of its members, who does not contribute to it in one way or another, according to his strength, his intellect, or his particular aptitudes; one does such a thing, another something else; but the action of each is profitable to all, and the action of all is profitable to each. Whether there be little or much, they share like brothers; around the domestic fireside no distinctions exist. Starvation is not perceived to sit there by the side of abundance. The cup, which God fills with His gifts, passes from hand to hand; and the aged man as well as the little child, he who cannot endure fatigue any longer, as well as he who cannot endure it yet; and he who returns from the field, his brow bathed with perspiration—all indiscriminately bring that cup to their lips. Their joys, their sufferings, are all common. If one among them is infirm, if he is taken ill, if he becomes unfit for labor before old age is there, the others provide for and take care of him, so that he is never abandoned.

There, where only one interest exists, no competition is possible; from that moment no discussions can occur. That which gives birth to dissensions, hatred and envy, is the insatiable desire of ever possessing more and more, when one possesses for one's self alone. Providence accurses those individual possessions. They continually irritate covetousness, and never gratify it. Those blessings alone do we really enjoy, which we share with others.

Father, mother, children, brothers, sisters, are there names saintlier and sweeter than those? and for what reason are there any other names on earth?

If those ties had been preserved such as they were primitively, we never would have known the greater part of the evils which afflict the human race, and sympathy would have alleviated those evils which are unavoidable. Those tears alone are composed of unmixed bitterness, which drop down on no one's bosom, and which no one wipes away.

Whence does it come that our destiny is so burdensome, and our life so full of miseries? Let us lay the fault upon none but ourselves; we have been unmindful of the laws of nature, we have deviated from its beaten path. He who parts with his traveling companions, in order to climb up amongst the rocks without assistance, must not complain if the ascent is rough.

Behold the fowls of the air; for they sow not, neither do they reap, nor gather into barns; yet your heavenly Father feedeth them. Are ye not much better than they?

There is room for all of us on this earth, and God has rendered it fertile enough that it may abundantly provide for the wants of all. Therefore, if a great many of our fellow-creatures want what is necessary to live, it is because man has disturbed the order, established by God; it is because he has destroyed the unity of the primitive family; it is because the members of that family have first become strangers to one another, and afterward enemies to one another.

Multitudes of particular societies, clans, tribes and nations have formed themselves, which, instead of protecting one another, had no other thought but of injuring one another.

All the wicked passions which arise from selfishness—and selfishness itself—have armed brothers against brothers; each has sought his own interest at the expense of others; rapine has banished security from the world; war has devastated it. They have furiously contended for the bloody fragments of the common inheritance. When strength now

—which was destined for labor which produces— is nearly entirely employed for destruction; when conflagrations, plunder and murder show man's passage over the earth; when conquest overthrows the natural relations between each population and the space of territory which it occupies and is able to cultivate; when numberless obstacles interrupt or stop the communications between one country and another country, and the free exchange of their productions;—is it otherwise possible but that disorders of so profound a nature should not give birth to sufferings equally profound?

The nations thus set at variance amongst themselves, each nation, moreover, has brought discord into itself. Some men have arisen, who uttered this impious word: We alone have a right to command and to govern; the others have no business but to obey.

They have made the laws in their benefit, and maintained them by force. On one side: power, wealth and enjoyment; on the other side: the whole burden of society.

In certain times and in certain countries, man has become the property of man; they have trafficked in man, they have sold him, they have bought him like a beast of burden.

In other countries and in other times, without depriving him of his liberty, they have done in such a manner that the fruit of his labor was almost entirely appropriated by those who held him under their dependency. Better would have been for him a state of complete slavery; for the master at least feeds, lodges and clothes his slave, and takes care of him when he is sick, on account of the interest he has in preserving him; but he who belongs to no one, they make use of him as long as there is any profit to get out of him, and then they throw him aside. What else might he be good for, when old age and labor have worn out his strength, but to die of hunger and cold at the corner of a street? Yet, even the very sight of him might give offense to those who enjoy all the pleasures of life. It is possible that on seeing them pass by, he might ask of them: A piece of bread, for the sake of God! That would not be agreeable to hear. And so it happens that they pick him up, and throw him into one of those filthy places which they call POOR-HOUSES, and which are like the approach to a dung-hill.

Everywhere, the excessive love of self has extinguished the love of others. Brothers have said to their brothers: We are not of the same lineage as you; our blood is purer; we do not wish to mingle with yours. You and your offspring, you are forever destined to serve us.

Elsewhere, they have established distinctions not on birth, but on money.

How much are you worth?

So much.

That is right; sit down at the social banquet, the table is spread for you. As for you who possess nothing, get you gone!

Does there exist a fatherland for the poor man?

And thus it is that wealth has marked the ranks and established the classes; they have had prerogatives of all kinds because they were rich; the exclusive privilege of having a share in the administration of the affairs of all, that is to say—of doing their own business at the expense of all, or nearly all.

The PROLETARIANS, as they are called with a superb disdain, although individually enfranchised, have been collectively the property of those who rule the relations between the members of society, the movement of industry, the conditions of labor, its price, and the partition of its fruits. What it has pleased them to ordain, they have called LAW; and the greater part of those laws have been nothing better than measures of private interest, means for the augmenting and perpetuating of domination, and the abuses of the domination of the smaller number over the greater number.

And that is what has become of the world, when the tie of fraternity was broken: Repose and opulence, and all the advantages on one side; whereas, on the other side, nothing but fatigue and misery, and the Potter's field at the end.

The former, under different names, constitute what is called the higher classes of society; the latter form what is called the people.

XX.

SOCIETY, ITS PAST, PRESENT AND FUTURE.

PART II.

You are the people. In the first place, you should know who are the people.

There are men who, bent under the burden of the day, incessantly exposed to the sun, the rain, the wind and all the inclemencies of the seasons, till the ground, deposit into its bosom, beside the seed which shall bear fruit, a part of their strength and of their life, and in this manner obtain from it, by the sweat of their face, the food which is necessary to all.

Those men are men of the people.

Others fell the forests; work the quarries and the mines; descend to immense depths in the bowels of the earth, in order to extract from it salt, coal, mineral ore and all the materials indispensable to trades and arts. These, as well as the former, grow old in rough labor, with the purpose of procuring for all the things which all need.

These, also, are men of the people.

Others melt the metals, mould them, and fashion them into shapes, which render them fit for a thousand various uses; there are others who work in wood; others weave the wool, the flax, the silk, and manufacture cloths of all kinds; others in the same manner provide for the different necessities which spring either directly from nature, or from the social condition.

These, likewise, are men of the people.

Many, amidst continual perils, travel over the seas for the purpose of transporting the peculiar productions of one country to other countries; or, they struggle against waves and tempests under the scorching sun of the tropics, as well as amidst the polar icebergs, either to the end of increasing the common stock by fishing, or in order to wrest from the ocean a multitude of productions, useful to human life.

These, equally, are men of the people.

And, who take up arms for their country, who defend her, who sacrifice to her the most beautiful years of their life, their vigils, yea, even their blood! who devote themselves and die for the security of others, in order to warrant them the quiet enjoyment of the domestic fireside, if not the children of the people?

And there are some among them who, across a thousand obstacles, pushed on, and sustained by their genius, develop and perfect the arts, letters and the sciences, which refine the morals, civilize the nations, surround them with that brilliant splendor, called glory, and in a word—constitute the most fertile among all sources of public prosperity.

And thus it is that in every country, all those who toil and drudge in order to bring forth and to spread the productions; all those whose labor turns to the profit of the whole community; the classes which are the most useful to its welfare and the most indispensable to its conservation, are none else but—the people. Take away a small number of privileged persons, buried in mere enjoyment, and the people is all mankind.

Without the people, all prosperity, all development, all life would be impossible; for, without work no life is possible, and work is everywhere the portion allotted to the people.

If the people suddenly disappeared, what would become of society? Society would disappear with it. There would be left only a few rare individuals, scattered over the land, who thereupon would be obliged to cultivate it with their own hands. In order to live, they would immediately be compelled to become the people themselves.

The question now which arises, is this: In that society, which is almost entirely composed of the people, and which only subsists through the people, what is the people's condition? what does that society do for the people?

It condemns them to struggle incessantly against multitudes of obstacles of all kinds, which it opposes to the amelioration of their lot, to the alleviation of their hardships; leaving to them but a scanty portion of the fruit of their labor; it treats the people like the ploughman treats his horse and his ox, and oftentimes a great deal worse; under different names it constantly proclaims: A servitude without end, and a wretchedness without hope!

XX.

SOCIETY, ITS PAST, PRESENT AND FUTURE.

PART III.

IF it were possible to compute all the sufferings which, for centuries and centuries, the people have undergone on the surface of the globe, not in consequence of the laws of Nature, but through the vices of Society, the number would be equal to the grass-blades, covering that earth, which is moistened with their tears.

Will such, then, for ever be the case? Is that multitude, then, doomed to go perpetually through the same circle of afflictions? Have they nothing to expect from the future? On all the points of their road, traced through the immensity of time, shall we, then, never hear anything else spring from their hearts but that one mournful cry of distress?

Is there really, then, within or without them, some fatal necessity which must forbid them a better condition until the end? Has God in heaven, then, condemned them to suffer in the same manner for ever and ever?

Throw it from you, that thought. That would be as if you blasphemed within yourselves.

The ways of God are ways of love. That which proceeds from Him, are not the evils which afflict those poor creatures, but the blessings which He scatters around them with profusion.

The gentle, tepid breeze which revives them in spring, is His breath; and the dew which refreshes them during the burning heat of summer, is His moist respiration.

There are some who say: On coming into this world, you are predestined to be tortured; here below, your life is and can be no other. But the real tortures are those who create them, and because they have established their welfare on no other foundation than the misfortunes of others, they should like to persuade them that their wretchedness is irremediable, and that even to try to get out of it, would be an attempt as criminal, as it is senseless.

Do not listen to such false reasonings. It is true,

perfect felicity to which every human being aspires, is not of this world; we pass through it, in order to attain an object, to perform our duties, and to accomplish a work; our repose will be on the other side only, and the present is the time to labor. That labor, however, pursuant to the design of Him who imposes it, cannot be meant to be a continual chastisement; but on the contrary, as much as the efforts to which it obliges us will allow, that labor, although a mixed happiness, may be a real blessing to us, a commencement of the joy, in which shall consist the reward of achievement.

We are like the ploughman: He sows at the beginning of winter, and does not reap before autumn. Yet, who would call his fatigue entirely unproductive of pleasure, for does not contentment spring up in his furrows in the same time with hope?

The remedy for that wretchedness, which they try to make you believe is incurable, rests with yourselves; and since the obstacle is not in Nature, but in Man, you will be able to remove it as soon as you wish; for those who misunderstand their own interest, and would try to prevent you from removing it, what is their strength in comparison to yours? You number a hundred against every one of theirs!

If up to the present, you have reaped so little fruit by your efforts, how can you be astonished at it? You held in your hands that which overthrows, and you had not in your hearts that which builds up; sometimes justice was not on your side; charity never was.

You had to defend your rights; you yourselves, or those who made use of your name, have often attacked the rights of others. It was incumbent upon you to establish FRATERNITY on earth, the Kingdom of God and the reign of Love. Instead of that, every one of you has thought of himself alone; every one of you had no other interest in view but his own; hatred and envy have inspired you. Search to the bottom of your hearts, and almost everyone of you will find there this secret thought: I toil and suffer; that man does nothing and swims in enjoyment; wherefore he rather than I? and the desire which you foster, is to be in his place, so that you might live and behave as he does.

That, now, would not be to exterminate the evil, but to perpetuate it. The evil consists in the injustice, and not in its being rather you than I who profit by the injustice.

Do you wish to succeed? Do that which is good

through good means alone. Do not confound the force which is directed by justice and charity, with the ferocious violence of the brute.

Do you wish to succeed? So think of your brothers as of yourselves; that their cause be your cause; their interest your interest; their distress your distress; see and feel yourselves only in them; let your indifference be transformed into a profound sympathy, and your self-love into self-sacrifice. And if you do so, you shall not be any longer scattered individuals, with whom a few, who are better united, do whatever they please; you shall be one, and the day on which you shall be one, you shall be all; and who hereafter shall dare to interpose himself between you and the object you wish to attain? Isolated, as you are standing at present, because every one of you bestows attention upon himself alone and his personal pursuits, they set you in opposition the one to the other; they subdue you the one through the other; but when you all shall have one and the same interest, one and the same will, the day that one and the same end shall be pursued by you all—where is the power that will be able to vanquish you?

But it is most essential that you should well

understand in what your task consists, or else all your efforts will prove abortive.

Your task is not to create yourselves individually a better lot, for in that case the great majority would remain suffering in the same manner, and nothing would be changed in the world; good and evil would continue in the same proportion, and as they concern the individual, they would only be distributed in a different way; there where you rise, another would go down, and that would be the only result.

Your task is not to substitute one domination for another domination. What does it matter who rules? All domination implies: distinct classes; consequently, privileges; consequently, an assemblage of interests which continually clash against one another; and in consequence of the laws, made by the higher classes to secure the advantages of their superior position, the immolation of all, or nearly all, to a few. The people is like the soil of the earth, where all those different classes take root.

But the task which is incumbent upon you, is this, it is a great one: You have to form the UNIVERSAL FAMILY; to build the City of God; to realize progressively, by an uninterrupted course of effort, His work in humanity.

And, when loving one another like brothers, you shall mutually treat one another like brothers; when each of you, seeking his happiness in the happiness of all, shall unite his life to the life of all, and his interests to the interests of all, ready at any moment to sacrifice himself for all the members of the common family, who in their turn are ready to sacrifice themselves for him—the greater part of the evils, under the burden of which the human race is groaning, will disappear, like the mists, which veil the horizon, are dispelled on the rising of the sun; and the will of God will be accomplished, for His will is: That Love, gradually uniting the scattered elements of mankind in a manner ever and ever more intimate, and organizing them into one body, shall make all mankind One, as He Himself is One.

XXI.

THE CITY OF SATAN AND THE CITY OF GOD.

The evils which afflict the earth come not from God, for God is love, and all that He has made, is good; they come from Satan, whom God has accursed, and from those men who have Satan for father and for a master.

Now, the children of Satan are numerous in the world. In order as they pass by, God records their names in a sealed book, which will be opened and read before all at the end of time.

There are men who love only themselves; and these are men of hatred, for to love one's self alone, is to hate others.

There are men of pride, who can endure no equals, who always wish to command and domineer.

There are men of covetousness, who constantly cry for gold, for honors, for pleasures, and are never satisfied.

There are men of rapine, who lie in wait for the feeble to despoil him by force or by cunning, and who spy by night around the dwelling of the widow and of the orphan.

There are men of crime, who have only vicious thoughts, who say: You are our brothers, and kill those whom they call their brothers, as soon as they suspect them to be opposed to their designs, and in their blood write the law.

There are men of fear, who tremble before the

wicked and kiss his hand, hoping thus to escape from his oppression, and who when one innocent is attacked on the public square, hasten to return home, and make fast their door.

All those men have destroyed peace, safety and liberty upon the earth.

You will then restore liberty, safety, peace, only by struggling against them without ceasing.

The City which they have founded, is the City of Satan; you have to rebuild the City of God.

In the City of God, each loves his brother as himself, and that is why no one is forsaken, no one suffers there, if there be a remedy for his sufferings.

In the City of God, all are equal, no one domineers, for justice reigns alone there with love.

In the City of God, each possesses his own without fear, and desires nothing more, because that which each has, is for all, and because all possess God, who unites in Himself all riches.

In the City of God, no one sacrifices others to himself, but each stands ready to sacrifice himself for others.

In the City of God, should a wicked person creep in, all shun him and all unite to restrain him, or to drive him out: for the wicked is the enemy of each, and the enemy of each is the enemy of all.

When you shall have rebuilt the City of God, the earth will bloom again, and the nations will flourish anew, because you will have overcome the children of Satan, who oppress the nations and lay waste the earth, the men of pride, the men of rapine, the men of slaughter and the men of fear.

XXII.

THE SEVEN KINGS.

PART I.

It was a dark night; a sky without stars hung above the earth, like a cover of black marble over a tomb.

And nothing disturbed the stillness of that night, but a strange noise, like a feeble flapping of wings, which from time to time was heard over the fields and the cities;

And then the darkness grew thicker, and every one felt his heart compressed, and a shivering run through his veins.

And in a hall, draped in black, and illumined by a reddish light, seven men, clothed in purple, their heads encircled with crowns, sat on seven seats of iron.

And in the midst of the hall was erected a throne, composed of dead men's bones, and at the foot of the throne was an overthrown crucifix for a footstool; before the throne stood a table of ebony, and on the table a vase, filled with red, frothing blood, and a human skull.

And the seven crowned men seemed pensive and sad, and their eyes, from the bottom of their sunken sockets, let now and then escape flashes of livid fire.

And one among them, having arisen, approached the throne with tottering step, and placed his foot on the crucifix.

In that moment, his limbs trembled, and he seemed on the point of swooning. The others fixed their gaze steadfastly upon him; they moved not, but I know not what passed over their brow, and a smile, not human, contracted their lips.

And he who had seemed on the point of swooning, stretched out his hand, seized the vase, filled with blood, poured part of it into the skull, and drank.

And that draught seemed to strengthen him.

And throwing back his head, this cry issued from his breast, like a death-rattle:

Accursed be Christ, who has brought back to earth Liberty!

And the six other crowned men arose together, and together rent the air with the same cry:

Accursed be Christ, who has brought back to earth Liberty!

Whereupon, sitting down again upon their seats of iron, the first said:

Brothers, what shall we do in order to extinguish Liberty? For our reign is at an end, if His begins. Our cause is the same: let each propose what he deems fitting.

As for me, this is the advice which I give. Before Christ came, who stood erect before us? It is His religion which has ruined us: let us abolish the religion of Christ.

And all answered: It is true. Let us abolish the religion of Christ.

And a second moved forward towards the throne, took the human skull, poured blood into it, drank, and thereupon spoke:

It is not religion only which we must abolish, but science and thought also; for science seeks to understand that, which is not good for us that man should know, and thought is always ready to resist authority.

And all answered: It is true. Let us abolish science and thought.

And having done as the two first, a third spoke:

When we shall have replunged men into brutishness, by taking away from them religion, and science, and thought, we shall have done a great deal, but something more will remain to be done.

The brute has instincts and dangerous sympathies. I will that no nation hear the voice of another nation, lest if the one begins to complain and grow restless, others be tempted to follow its example. That no rumor from abroad penetrate among us.

And all answered: It is true. That no rumor from abroad penetrate among us.

And a fourth said: We have our interest, and the nations have their interest likewise, opposed to ours. If they unite against us to defend that interest, how shall we resist them?

Let us divide in order to reign. Let us create in each province, in each town, in each hamlet, an interest opposed to that of every other hamlet, every other town, and every other province.

So, each shall hate the other, and they shall not think of uniting against us.

And all answered: It is true. Let us divide in order to reign: concord would kill us.

And a fifth having twice filled with blood, and twice emptied the human skull, spoke:

I approve all these means, they are good, but insufficient. Make brutes, that is well; but frighten those brutes, strike them with terror, by means of an inexorable justice and atrocious penalties, if you do not wish to be devoured by them sooner or later. The executioner is the first minister of a good prince.

And all answered: It is true. The executioner is the first minister of a good prince.

And a sixth said:

I admit the advantage of sudden, terrible, inevitable penalties. Yet, there exist strong minds and desperate, who brave all penalties.

Do you wish to govern men easily, enervate them through voluptuousness. Virtue does nothing for us; it begets strength: let us rather exhaust it through corruption.

And all answered: It is true. Let us exhaust strength, and energy, and courage through corruption.

Then, the seventh, having like the others drunk from the human skull, spoke in this manner, his feet resting on the crucifix:

Christ is abolished; there is war unto death, eternal war between Him and us.

But how shall we detach from Him the people? That is a vain attempt. What shall we do then? Listen: we must buy the priests of Christ with wealth, honors and power.

And they shall command the people, in the name of Christ, to be entirely submissive to us, whatever we may do, whatever we may prescribe;

And the people will believe them, and will obey through conscience, and our authority shall be more firmly established than before.

And all answered: It is true. Let us corrupt the priests of Christ.

And suddenly the light, which illumined the hall, went out, and the seven men separated in darkness.

And to one righteous who, at that moment, waked and prayed before the cross, these words were spoken: My day approaches. Adore and fear nothing.

XXII.

THE SEVEN KINGS.

PART II.

AND through a gray and dense fog, I saw, as is seen on earth at the hour of twilight, a plain, naked, desolate and cold.

In the midst arose a rock, from which trickled down drop by drop blackish water, and the feeble and dull noise of the drops as they fell, was the only noise heard.

And seven foot-paths, after winding through the plain, came to the foot of the rock, and near the rock, at the entrance of each, was a stone, covered with I know not what of slime and green, like the slaver of a reptile.

And behold, in one of the paths, I perceived something like a shade which moved forward slowly; and gradually the shade coming nearer, I discerned, not a man, but the resemblance of a man.

And in the region of the heart, this human form had a stain of blood.

And it sat down upon the stone slimy and green, and its limbs shivered, and inclining its head, it wrapped itself in its arms, as if to retain a remnant of heat.

And by the six other paths, six other shades successively arrived at the foot of the rock.

And each of them, shivering and wrapping itself in its arms, sat down upon the stone slimy and green.

And they sat there, silent and oppressed under the weight of some incomprehensible anguish.

And their silence lasted a long time, I know not how long, for the sun never rises on that plain: it knows neither evening nor morning. The drops of black water there, in falling, alone measure a lapse of time, monotonous, dismal, terrible, eternal.

And that was so horrible to see, that if God had not strengthened me, I should not have been able to endure the sight.

And, after a sort of convulsive shuddering, one of the shades, raising its head, sent forth a sound, like the hoarse, dry sound of the wind, whistling through a skeleton.

And the rock echoed these words to my ear:

Christ has conquered: accursed be He!

And the six other shades shuddered, and all at the same time raising their heads, the same blasphemy issued from their breasts:

Christ has conquered: accursed be He!

And immediately they were seized with a stronger shuddering, the fog grew more dense, and for a moment, the black water ceased to flow.

And the seven shades had bent down again under the burden of their secret anguish, and there was a second silence, longer than the first.

Thereupon one of them, without rising from its seat, motionless and with its head inclined, said to the others:

The same, then, which befell me, has befallen you. Of what use to us have been all our counsels!

And another said: Faith and thought have broken the chains of the people; faith and thought have enfranchised the earth.

And another said: we wished to divide men, and our oppression has united them against us.

And another: we have shed blood, and that blood has risen up against us.

And another: We have sown corruption, and it has germinated in us, and it has consumed the marrow of our bones.

And another: We meant to extinguish Liberty, and its breath has withered our power even to the root.

Then the seventh shade:
Christ has conquered: accursed be He!
And all, of one accord, exclaimed:
Christ has conquered: accursed be He!

And I saw a hand come forward; it dipped its finger into the blackish water, whose drops, in falling, measure eternal time, marked with it the foreheads of the seven shades, and this was forever.

XXIII.

ALL ARE BORN EQUAL.

You have but one Father, who is God, and but one Master, who is Christ.

When, therefore, they shall tell you of those, who possess on earth great power: Behold your masters, believe it not. If they are just, they are your servants; if they are not, they are your tyrants.

All are born equal: no one, in coming into this world, brings with him the right to command.

I have seen in a cradle a child, crying and dreuling, and around it were old men, who called it: Lord, and who, falling upon their knees, adored it. And I have understood all the misery of man.

It is sin which has made princes; because, instead

of loving and aiding one another as brothers, men began by injuring one another.

Then, from among themselves, they chose one or several, whom they thought the most just, to protect the good from the wicked, and so that the feeble might live in peace.

And the power they wielded, was a legitimate power, for it was the power of God, who wills that justice reign, and the power of the people who had elected them.

And therefore every one was bound in conscience to obey them.

But very soon there were also found men, who wished to reign in their own right, as if they were of a nature, loftier, than their brothers.

And the power of these is not legitimate, for it is the power of Satan, and their domination is the domination of pride and cupidity.

And this is the reason, that unless greater evil will result, every one may and sometimes ought to, in conscience, resist them.

In the balance of eternal justice, your will weighs more than the will of kings; for it is the people who make kings; and kings are made for the people, and the people are not made for kings.

The heavenly Father has not moulded the limbs of His children to be bruised by fetters, nor their soul to be crushed by servitude.

He has united them in families, and all families are brothers; He has united them in nations, and all nations are brothers; and whosoever parts family from family, nation from nation, divides what God has united: he does the work of Satan.

And that which unites family to family, nation to nation, is in the first place the law of God, the law of justice and of fraternity, and then the law of liberty, which is also the law of God.

For, without liberty, what union would exist among men? They would be united as the horse is united to his rider, as the rod of the master to the skin of the slave.

If, therefore, any one comes and says: You are mine; reply: No; we belong to God, who is our Father, and to Christ, who is our only Master.

XXIV.

DUMB ANIMALS AND INTELLIGENT ANIMALS.

The people are incapable of understanding their interests; for their own welfare, they ought always to be kept in tutelage. Is it not the part of those who have knowledge, to guide those who have no knowledge?

So say many hypocrites who wish to administer the affairs of the people, to the end of growing fat on the substance of the people.

You are incapable, they say, of understanding your interests; and thereupon, they will not even allow you to dispose of what is your own, for a purpose you deem useful; and they will dispose of it, against your will, for another purpose which displeases and is repugnant to you.

You are incapable of managing a petty property in common, incapable of understanding what is good or bad for you, of knowing your own needs and providing for them; and thereupon, they will send you men, well-paid at your expense, who will govern your estate to their fancy, prevent you from doing what you wish, and compel you to act against your wishes.

You are incapable of discerning what education is proper for your children; and in tenderness for your children, they will cast them into sinks of impiety and bad morals, unless you should prefer to deprive them of every kind of instruction.

You are incapable of judging whether or not, you and your family can subsist on the salary they allow you for your labor; and they will forbid you, under severe penalties, from concerting together to obtain an increase of that salary, that you may live, you, your wives, and your children.

If what this race of greed and hypocrisy says, were true, you would be far beneath the brute, for the brute knows all they assert that you do not know, and the brute knows it by instinct alone.

God has not made you to be the herd of a few other men. He has made you to live free, in society, as brothers. Now, a brother has no right to command his brother. Brothers unite among themselves by mutual consent, and that consent is law, and law must be respected, and all should join to prevent its violation, because it is the safeguard of all, the will and the interest of all.

Be men: no one is powerful enough to bend you to the yoke against your will; but you can offer your neck to the bow yourselves, if you wish.

There are stupid animals who stand in the stall, who are fed for labor, and then, when they grow old, are fattened for food.

There are others that live at large on the plain,

that cannot be bent to servitude, that do not suffer themselves to be seduced by deceitful caresses, nor to be subdued by threats and ill-usage.

The brave resemble the last: the cowardly are like the first.

XXV.

LIBERTY.

LEARN then, how to make yourselves free.

To be free, it is above all necessary to love God, for if you love God, you will do His will; and the will of God is justice and fraternity, without which there is no liberty.

When, by violence or through craft, one takes away what belongs to another; when one attacks him in his person; when, in a lawful matter, one prevents him from acting as he wishes, or when one compels him to act contrary to his wish; when one violates his right in any manner soever, what is that? An injustice. It is therefore injustice which destroys liberty.

If each loved himself alone, and thought only of himself, without aiding others, the poor man would be obliged frequently to take away what belongs to another, that he may live and support his family; the feeble would be oppressed by one stronger, and he by another still more strong; injustice would reign everywhere. Fraternity, then, preserves liberty.

Love God above all things, and thy neighbor as thyself, and servitude will disappear from the earth.

Those, however, who profit by the servitude of their brothers, will do all in their power to continue it. To that end they will employ falsehood and power.

They will tell you that the absolute authority of a few and the slavery of all others is the established order of God; and to maintain their tyranny, they will not fear to blaspheme Providence.

Reply to them: that such a God, their God, is Satan, the enemy of the human race, and that your God is He, who has vanquished Satan.

Thereupon, they will let loose upon you their satellites; they will construct prisons without number to confine you in; they will persecute you with fire and sword; they will torture you and shed your blood as the water from the fountain.

If, therefore, you are not resolved to battle without ceasing, to suffer all things without blenching, to never grow weary, never to yield, remain in your fetters, and renounce a liberty of which you are not worthy.

Liberty is like the kingdom of God; it suffereth violence, and the violent take it by force.

And the violence which puts you in possession of liberty, is not the brutish violence of thieves and robbers, injustice, vengeance, barbarity; but a will, strong and inflexible, a courage, calm and generous.

The cause most holy changes into a cause, impious and execrable, when crime is employed to uphold it. From a slave, the man of crime may become a tyrant, but never will he become free.

XXVI.

THE PRAYER OF THE PROLETARIANS.

Lord, we cry unto Thee from the depths of our misery.

Like animals, who are in want of food to give to their young,

We cry unto Thee, Lord.

Like the ewe, from whom her lamb is taken,

We cry unto Thee, Lord.

Like the dove, seized by the vulture,

We cry unto Thee, Lord.
Like the gazelle, under the claw of the tiger,
We cry unto Thee, Lord.
Like the bull, exhausted with fatigue and scored by the goad,
We cry unto Thee, Lord.
Like the wounded bird, pursued by the dog,
We cry unto Thee, Lord.
Like the swallow, fallen with weariness, in crossing the sea, and struggling on the wave,
We cry unto Thee, Lord.
Like the traveler, lost in a desert, burning and destitute of water,
We cry unto Thee, Lord.
Like those shipwrecked on a barren coast,
We cry unto Thee, Lord.
Like him, who, at nightfall, encounters, near a church-yard, a hideous spectre,
We cry unto Thee, Lord.
Like the father, from whom is snatched the morsel of bread, he was taking to his starving children,
We cry unto Thee, Lord.
Like the prisoner, whom unjust power has thrown into a dungeon, damp and dark,
We cry unto Thee, Lord.

Like the slave, lacerated by the whip of his master,

We cry unto Thee, Lord.

Like the innocent, who is led to execution,

We cry unto Thee, Lord.

Like the people of Israel in the land of bondage,

We cry unto Thee, Lord.

Like the descendants of Jacob, whose men-children Egypt's king caused to be drowned in the Nile,

We cry unto Thee, Lord.

Like the twelve tribes, whose labors were every day increased by their oppressors, while each day their food was diminished,

We cry unto Thee, Lord.

Like all nations of the earth, before deliverance had dawned upon them,

We cry unto Thee, Lord.

Like Christ on the cross, when He cried: Father, Father, why hast Thou forsaken me?

We cry unto Thee, Lord.

Oh Father! Thou hast not forsaken Thy Son, Thy Christ, unless in appearance and for a moment only; so Thou wilt not abandon for ever the brothers of Christ. His divine blood, which has redeemed them from the bondage of the Prince of this world, will also redeem them from the bondage of the ministers of the Prince of this world. Behold their feet and their hands pierced, their side pierced, their head covered with bloody wounds. In the earth, which Thou hadst given for their heritage, a vast sepulchre has been dug for them, and they have been thrown therein, indiscriminately, and sealed has been the stone which covers it, with a seal, on which in mockery has been engraved Thy holy name. And thus, oh Lord, they lie there; but they will not lie there eternally. Three days more, and the sacrilegious seal will be broken, and the stone will be dashed in pieces, and those who sleep, will awake, and the reign of Christ, which is justice and fraternity, and peace and joy in the Spirit of God, will commence. So be it.

XXVII.

CHRIST AND THE PEOPLE.

Who thronged around Christ to hear His word? The people.

Who followed Him to the mountain and to the desert places to listen to His teachings? The people.

Who wished to make choice of Him for king? The people.

Who spread their garments and strewed palm-branches in His way, crying Hosanna, when He entered Jerusalem? The people.

Who were offended because of the sick whom He healed on a sabbath-day? The scribes and the Pharisees.

Who questioned Him with cunning, and laid snares to destroy Him? The scribes and the Pharisees.

Who said of Him: He is possessed? Who called Him a gluttonous man and a drinker of wine? The scribes and the Pharisees.

Who styled Him: leader of sedition and a blasphemer? who conspired against Him to put Him to death? who crucified Him on Calvary between two thieves?

The scribes and the Pharisees, the doctors of law, Herod the king and his courtiers, the Roman governor and the chief priests.

Their craft, full of hypocrisy, deceived the people themselves. They persuaded them to ask for the death of Him, who had fed them in the desert with seven loaves, restored health to the sick, sight to the blind, hearing to the deaf, and to the lame the use of their limbs.

But Jesus, seeing that they had beguiled the people, as the serpent beguiled the woman, prayed His Father, saying: Father, forgive them: for they know not what they do.

And yet, during eighteen centuries, the Father has not forgiven them, and they bend under their punishment over the whole earth, and in every part of the earth, the slave is constrained to bow his head to see them.

The mercy of Christ excludes no one. He came into this world to save not a few men, but all men; He has had for each of them a drop of blood.

But the small, the feeble, the meek, the poor, all those who suffered, He loved with a special love.

His heart beat to the heart of the people, and the heart of the people beat to His heart.

And it is there, on the heart of Christ, that the nations sick revive, and the nations oppressed receive strength to become free.

Woe unto those who forsake Him, who deny Him! Their wretchedness is without remedy, and their servitude without end.

XXVIII.

INTOLERANCE OF RELIGION.

The time has been, when man in cutting the throat of his fellow, whose faith differed from his own, believed that he offered a sacrifice, agreeable to God.

Let those horrible murders be an abomination to you.

How could the murder of man be pleasing to God, who has said to man: Thou shalt not kill?

When the blood of man flows upon the earth, as an offering to God, demons run to drink it, and enter into him who has spilled it.

One commences to persecute only when he despairs of convincing, and whoever despairs of convincing, either thinks blasphemy against the power of truth, or believes not in the truth of the doctrines which he teaches.

What is more insane than to say to men: Believe or die!

Faith is the daughter of the Word: she enters into the heart with persuasion, and not with the dagger.

Jesus went about, doing good, attracting by His

kindness, and touching with His sweetness souls the most hardened.

His divine lips blessed and cursed not, unless may be the hypocrites. He did not choose executioners for apostles.

He said to His own: Let both grow together until the harvest, the good and the bad seed; the householder shall make the separation on the thrashing-floor.

And to those who urged Him to cause fire from heaven to descend upon a city of unbelievers: Ye know not what manner of spirit ye are of.

The spirit of Jesus is a spirit of peace, of mercy and of love.

Those who carry on persecution in His name, who search conscience with the sword, who torture the body to convert the soul, who cause tears to flow, instead of wiping them away: such have not the spirit of Jesus.

Woe unto him who profanes the Gospel, making it to men an object of terror! Woe unto him who writes the glad tidings on a page in blood!

Remember the catacombs.

In that time, they dragged you to the scaffold; they gave you up to wild beasts in the amphitheatre to amuse the rabble; they cast you by thousands into deep mines and into prisons; they confiscated your goods; they trod you under foot like the mire of the streets; you had where to celebrate your proscribed worship no other asylum than the bowels of the earth.

What said your persecutors? They said that you propagated dangerous teachings; that your sect, as they called it, disturbed order and public peace; that you, violators of law and enemies of mankind, made the empire totter, in shattering the religion of the empire.

And in this distress, under this oppression, for what did you ask? liberty. You claimed the right of obeying only God, of serving Him, and of worshipping Him, according to your conscience.

When, although mistaken in their faith, others shall claim of you this sacred right, respect it in them, even as you demanded the heathens to respect it in you.

Respect it, that you may not dishonor the memory of the early Christians, and may not defile the ashes of your martyrs.

Persecution is two-edged: it wounds to the right and to the left.

If you are forgetful of Christ's teachings, remember the catacombs.

XXIX.

THE LAW OF CHRIST.

Treasure carefully within your souls justice and fraternity; they will be your safeguard they will destroy from among you discord and dissension.

That which creates discord and dissension, that which causes the suits at law which scandalize honest men, and ruin families, is before all niggardly self-interest, the insatiable passion of acquiring and of possessing.

Fight therefore without ceasing that passion within you, which Satan constantly arouses there.

What can you carry away of all the riches, which you shall have amassed by good and by bad means? Little suffices man, who lives so short a time.

Another cause of endless dissension is bad laws.

Now, there are but few laws in the world, other than bad.

What other law is necessary for him, who has the law of Christ?

The law of Christ is clear, it is holy, and there is

no person, if he have that law in his heart, who judges not himself easily.

Listen to what has been said to me:

The children of Christ, if they have among themselves any difference, must not carry it before the tribunals of those who oppress the earth and who corrupt it.

Are there not aged men among them? and are not those aged men their fathers, knowing justice and loving it?

Let them seek then one of those aged men, and say to him: Father, we have not been able to agree, my brother here and I; we beseech you, judge between us.

And the aged man will listen to the words of each, and he will judge between them, and having judged, he will bless them.

And if they submit to that judgment, the blessing will abide with them: if not, it will return to the aged man, who shall have pronounced the just judgment.

There is nothing impossible to those who are united, be it for good, be it for evil. The day, then, when you shall be united, will be the day of your deliverance.

When the children of Israel were oppressed in the land of Egypt, if each, forgetful of his brother, had wished to leave alone, no one of them would have escaped; they all departed together, and nothing could detain them.

You are also in the land of Egypt, bowed down under the sceptre of Pharaoh and under the whip of his taskmasters. Cry unto the Lord, your God, and thereupon arise, and go out together.

XXX.

FATHER AND SON.

Father, labor is wearisome to-day; the hoe rebounds from the parched earth; the sun darts rays of fire; swept by the wind of the south, the dust whirls over the plain.

My son, He who sends the burning blasts, sends also the rain-clouds. Each day has its sorrow and its hope, and after toil, rest.

Father, see those poor plants, how they languish, how their fading leaves droop along the stalk, bending beneath its own weight.

They will revive, my son; not a blade of grass is forgotten; there is always for it, among the treasures of heaven, fertilizing showers and refreshing dews.

Father, the birds are silent in the trees; the quail, motionless in the up-turned furrow, does not even call his mate; the heifer seeks the shade, and the bull, his legs bending under his bulky body, his neck extended, dilates his large nostrils to inhale the air which he needs.

My son, God will restore to the birds their voice, to the bulls and to the heifers their strength, exhausted by this burning heat. Already, across the waters, blows the breeze which will reanimate them.

Father, let us sit down upon the fern, at the edge of the pond, beside that aged oak, whose hanging branches touch lightly the surface of the water. How calm and transparent it is! How merrily the fishes sport there! Some pursue their winged prey, poor gnats that just commenced to live; others, raising up their head, seem with their mouth half open to give the air a light kiss.

My son, He who has made all things, has distributed everywhere His inexhaustible gifts, both existence and the joys of existence. Evil is but in appearance, the dark side of love, one face of good, its shadow.

Yet, father, what toil, what hardships you suffer, that you may provide for our wants! Are you not poor? Is mother not poor? It is in your sweat that I have been nourished; and for a single day have you been free from anxiety for the morrow?

Why think of the morrow, my son? To-morrow is for God; let us put our trust in Him. He who rises in the morning, knows not if he shall reach the evening. Why then be troubled and uneasy about a time which perhaps will never come? We pass here below like the swallow, seeking each day a daily subsistence, and like the swallow, when winter comes, a mysterious power draws us to climes more mild.

What is that, father? it seems like a dead body wrapped in its shroud, or a babe rolled in its swaddling-clothes?

My son, it was a creeping worm, it will soon be a living flower, an airy form, which, spangled with the most vivid hues, will mount toward the heavens.

XXXI.

THE FRUIT OF SIN.

The weather was sultry. A man perceived at the base of a hill a vine loaded with grapes, and that man was thirsty, and the desire came upon him to quench his thirst with the fruit of the vine.

But between it and him was spread out a muddy swamp which must be passed to reach the hill, and he lacked resolution.

Yet, his thirst urging, he said: It may be that the mire is not deep; who hinders me from attempting what so many others have done? I shall but soil my shoes, and the harm, after all, will not be great.

Thereupon, he steps into the swamp, his foot sinks into the foul mud, soon he sinks as far as his knee.

He stops, he hesitates, he asks himself: were it not better to return again? But the vine and its grapes are before him there, and he feels his thirst increase.

Since I have gone so far, why, says he, should I retrace my steps? Wherefore should I lose my labor? A little mud more or less, now, makes no difference. Besides, I shall only be put to the trouble of washing in the first brook.

That thought decides him; he goes forward, he advances farther, sinking always deeper and deeper into the mire; he sinks as far as his breast, then to his neck, then to his lips; it passes finally above his head. Smothering and gasping, a last effort extricates him and carries him to the foot of the hill.

Covered over with black slime, which runs down his limbs, he plucks the fruit so much coveted, he devours it. After which, ill at ease, ashamed of himself, he strips off his clothing, and searches on all sides for clear water to cleanse himself. But all in vain, the stench remains; the exhalation of the swamp has penetrated his flesh and his bones, it exudes from him continually and forms around him a fetid atmosphere. If he approaches, others rush away. People shun him. He has made himself a reptile, let him go and live among reptiles.

XXXII.

A LESSON FROM THE SWALLOWS.

ALL nature teaches us the indispensable need, in which we stand the one of the other; the divine precept of mutual assistance, of self-sacrifice and love is incessantly called to our minds by what we observe around us: When the time has come for them to go and look in other climates for the food, which the Father in heaven has there prepared for them, the swallows flock together. From that time, never once separating, little mariners of the air, they take their flight for the shore, where they will rest in peace and abundance. Starting each for itself alone, what would become of them? Not one would escape the perils of the road; united, they resist the winds; the feeble or fatigued wing leans against one that is stronger. Poor, sweet, little creatures, which last spring saw come to light, the youngest-born, protected by the elder ones, reach under their guard the term of their voyage, and on the far-distant shore, where Providence has guided them beyond the sea, they dream of their native nest and its first joys—those mysterious, inexpressible joys, which God, for all His beings, has placed at the entrance of life.

XXXIII.

MAN, HIS PAST, PRESENT AND FUTURE.

And I had seen the evils which were on earth, the feeble oppressed, the righteous begging his bread, the wicked raised to honors and rolling in wealth, the innocent condemned by iniquitous judges, and their children wandering under the sun.

And my soul was sad, and hope escaped from it on all sides, as from a broken vase.

And God wrapped me in profound sleep.

And in my sleep, I saw like a luminous shape, standing near me, a Spirit, whose sweet and piercing gaze penetrated even to the bottom of my most secret thoughts.

And I trembled, not in fear, nor in joy, but from a feeling which seemed, as it were, a strange mixture of both.

And the Spirit said to me: Why are you sad?

And weeping, I answered him: Oh! behold the evils which are on the earth.

And the celestial form smiled with an ineffable smile, and these words came to my ear:

Your eye sees nothing but through this deceitful medium, which creatures call time. Time is only for you: for God there is no time.

And I remained silent, for I understood not.

Look, said the Spirit suddenly.

And, without there existing thenceforth for me either before or after, in the same instant, I saw at once, what in their infirm and feeble language men call time, past, present and future.

And they were all one, and yet, in telling what I

saw, it is necessary for me to descend again to the limits of time, I must speak the infirm and feeble language of men.

And the whole human race seemed to me as one man.

And that man had done much evil, little good, had known many sorrows, few joys.

And he was there, groveling in his wretchedness, on a plain, now frozen, now burning hot, emaciated, starving, suffering, oppressed by alternate languor and convulsions, loaded with chains, forged in the abode of demons.

His right hand had wrapped them around his left hand, and the left hand had loaded the right, and during his terrible dreams, he had so entangled himself in his fetters, that his whole body was covered and distorted by them.

For whenever they simply touched him, they clung to his skin like molten lead, they entered into his flesh, and remained there.

And such was man; I knew him.

And, behold! a ray of Light proceeded from the East, and a ray of Love from the South, and a ray of Strength from the North.

And these three rays, united, touched on the heart of that man.

And as the ray of Light came forth, a voice said: Son of God, brother of Christ, know what thou shouldst know.

And as the ray of Love came forth, a voice said: Son of God, brother of Christ, love whom thou shouldst love.

And as the ray of Strength came forth, a voice said: Son of God, brother of Christ, do what should be done.

And when the three rays were united, the three voices were united also, and they formed a single voice, which said:

Son of God, brother of Christ, serve God, and serve Him alone.

And then, what had hitherto seemed to me as one man, appeared to be a multitude of peoples and of nations.

And my first look had not deceived me, nor did my second deceive me.

And those peoples and nations, awaking on their bed of agony, commenced to say among themselves:

Whence come our sufferings and our languor, and the hunger and the thirst which torment us, and the chains which weigh us down to the earth, and enter into our flesh?

And their mind was enlightened, and they understood that the sons of God, the brothers of Christ, had not been condemned by their Father to slavery, and that this slavery was the source of all their evils.

Each then attempted to break his fetters, but no one succeeded.

And they looked at one another with mutual pity, and love working in them, they said to one another: We have all the same thought, why should we not all have the same heart? Are we not all sons of the same God, and brothers of the same Christ? Let us free one another, or die together.

And having thus spoken, they felt within themselves a strength divine, and I heard their fetters crack, and they battled six days against those who held them in chains, and the sixth day they were victorious, and the seventh was a day of rest.

And the earth, which was dry, became green again, and all could eat of its fruits, and go and come, without any person saying to them: Whither do you go? no one passes here.

And the little children culled flowers, and brought them to their mothers, who smiled on them tenderly.

And there were neither poor nor rich, but all had in abundance the things, necessary to their wants, because all loved and assisted one another as brothers.

And a voice, like the voice of an angel, resounded through the heavens: Glory to God, who has given Intellect, Love and Strength to His children! Glory to Christ, who has restored to His brothers Liberty!

XXXIV.

THE REIGN OF SATAN.

And I was transported in spirit to ancient times, and the earth was beautiful, and rich, and fertile; and its inhabitants lived happy, because they lived as brothers.

And I saw the Serpent, which crawled among them: he fastened on many his potent gaze, and their soul was troubled, and they approached him, and the Serpent whispered in their ear.

And after having listened to the whisper of the Serpent, they rose up and said: We are kings.

And the sun grew pale, and the earth took on a funereal hue, like that of the shroud which enwraps the dead.

And there was heard a dull murmuring, a long lamentation, and the heart of each trembled.

Verily, I say unto you, it was like the day, when the fountains of the great deep were broken up, and when the deluge of the great waters spread itself abroad.

Fear ran from hut to hut, for as yet there were no palaces, and in secret it spoke to each things, which made him shudder.

And those who had said: We are kings, seized a sword, and followed Fear from hut to hut.

And strange mysteries took place there; and there were chains, tears and blood.

The men, terrified, cried aloud: Murder has appeared again on earth. And this was all, because Fear had benumbed their courage and paralyzed their arms.

And they suffered themselves to be loaded with chains, themselves, and their wives, and their children. And those who had said: We are kings, dug out a pit, like a great cavern, and in it they confined the whole human race, even as one shuts up animals in a stable.

And the tempest swept the clouds onward, and the thunder rolled, and I heard a voice which said:

The Serpent has conquered a second time, but not for always.

After that, I heard nothing more but confused voices, laughter, groans and blasphemies.

And I knew that there must be a reign of Satan, before the reign of God. And I wept, and I had hope.

And the vision which I saw, was true, for the reign of Satan is accomplished, and the reign of God will be accomplished also, and those who have said: We are kings, will be in their turn confined in the cavern with the Serpent, and the human race will come forth from it, and it will be for them like a new birth, like the passage from death to life. So let it be.

XXXV.

THE WAR BETWEEN CAPITAL AND LABOR.

Every thing that takes place in this world, is preceded by an omen.

When the sun is about to rise, the horizon is tinged with a thousand shades, and the East appears on fire.

When the tempest comes, a dull roar is heard on the shore, and the waves are as if self-tossed.

The thoughts numberless and diverse, which meet and mingle at the horizon of the spiritual world, are the omen which announces the rising of the sun of intelligence.

The confused murmur and the internal workings of the people in excitement are the omen, preceding the tempest which will soon pass over the quaking nations.

Be ye therefore ready, for the time is at hand.

In that day, there will be great terror, and cries such as have not been heard since the days of the deluge.

The kings will shriek upon their thrones; with both hands they will seek to retain their crowns from being blown away by the winds, and with their crowns they themselves will be swept away.

The rich and the powerful will flee naked from their palaces, for fear of being buried under the ruins.

They will be seen, wandering on the highways, begging the passers-by for rags to cover their nakedness, and for a crust of bread to appease their hunger, and I know not that they will obtain it.

And there will be men, who shall be seized with thirst for blood, and who will worship death, and who will advocate its worship.

And death will stretch forth his bony hand as if to bless them, and that benediction will fall upon their heart, and it will cease to beat.

And the wise will grow troubled in their wisdom, and it will seem to them as a small spot of darkness, when the sun of intelligence shall arise.

And in proportion as it ascends, its warmth will melt away the clouds, heaped up by the tempest; and they will be only as a thin vapor, which the zephyrs chase toward the West.

Never will the sky have been so serene, nor the earth so green and so fertile.

And instead of the feeble twilight that we call day, a light strong and pure will shine on high, like a reflection from the face of God.

And in that light men will behold themselves, and will say: We knew neither ourselves, nor our neighbors; we had no idea of man. Now, we know.

And each in his brother will love himself, and find his happiness in serving him; and there will be neither small nor great, because of the love which makes all equal, and all families will be as one family, and all nations as one nation.

This is the reading of the mystic letters, which the Jews in their blindness affixed to the cross of Christ.

XXXVI.

THE SECOND COMING OF CHRIST.

LISTEN attentively, and tell me whence comes this confused sound, vague and strange, which is heard on all sides.

Place your hand on the earth, and tell me why it trembles.

Something, we know not what, moves in the world: a travail of God is going on there.

Is every one not in expectation? Is there one heart that does not beat?

Child of man, mount the heights, and tell what you see.

I see in the horizon a livid cloud, and around it a red light, like the reflection of a fire.

Child of man, what do you see more?

I see the ocean toss its waves, and the mountains shake their peaks.

I see the rivers change their course, the hills totter, and in falling fill the valleys.

Every thing reels, every thing moves, every thing takes on a new appearance.

Child of man, what more do you see?

I see whirlwinds of dust in the distance, and they sweep in all directions, and they rush together, and mingle, and are lost in each other. They pass over the cities, and when they have passed, they leave naught but a plain.

I see the nations rise in tumult, and the kings grow pale 'neath their diadem. There is war between them, a war unto death.

I see a throne, two thrones, broken in pieces, and the nations scatter the fragments over the earth.

I see a nation battle, as the archangel Michael battled against Satan. Its blows are terrible, but it is naked, and its enemy is covered with massive armor.

Oh God! it falls; it is stricken to death. No, it is only wounded. Mary, the Virgin-Mother, wraps it up in her cloak, smiles on it, and carries it away for a time out of the battle.

I see another nation struggle without cessation, and revive from time to time its strength in that struggle. That nation has the sign of Christ on its heart.

I see a third nation, on which six kings have placed their foot, and every time it moves, six poniards are plunged into its throat.

I see over a vast building, very high in the air,

a cross which I can scarcely distinguish, because it is covered with a black veil.

Child of man, what else do you see?

I see the Orient, which is troubled in itself. It sees its ancient palaces crumble, its old temples fall to dust, and it raises its eyes as if in search of other grandeurs and another God.

I see towards the Occident a woman with proud eye, with serene brow; she traces with firm hand a light furrow, and wherever the plowshare passes, I see human generations spring up, who invoke her in their prayers, and bless her in their songs.

I see in the North men who have nothing but a remnant of warmth, concentrated in their brain, and which intoxicates it; but Christ touches them with His cross, and the heart commences to beat again.

I see in the South races, overwhelmed in I know not what curse: a heavy yoke weighs them down, they walk bent over; but Christ touches them with His cross, and they rise erect.

Child of man, what more do you see?

He answers not; let us cry again.

Child of man, what do you see?

I see Satan who flees, and Christ, surrounded with His angels, who comes to reign.

XXXVII.

THE MIGHTY OF EARTH.

I saw a beech raise aloft its head to a wondrous height. From its summit nearly to its root, it threw out enormous branches, which so overshadowed the earth on all sides, that it was barren; not a single blade of grass would grow there. At the foot of the forest-giant sprang up an oak which, after growing up a few feet, bent over, twisted itself, grew out horizontally, then rose again and twisted itself anew; and finally it was seen stretching forth its sickly and leafless head from beneath the vigorous branches of the beech, in search of a little air and a little light.

And to myself I thought: thus grow the small in the shadow of the great.

Who gather around the powerful of the world? Who draw near them? not the poor man; they drive him away: his appearance would offend their eyes. With care they banish him from their presence and from their palaces; they permit him not even to pass through their parks, open to all, except him, because his body, worn with toil, is clad in the garments of poverty.

Who then gather around the powerful of the world? the rich and the flatterers who desire power, the degraded women, the infamous panders of their private pleasures, the ballet-dancers, the buffoons who lull, and the false prophets who delude their conscience.

Who besides? the violent, the crafty, the agents of oppression, the usurers, all those who say: Deliver to us the people, and we will pour their gold into your coffers and their substance into your veins.

Where lies the carcass, there the vultures will gather.

The little birds build their nest in the grass, and the birds of prey in lofty trees.

XXXVIII.

THE PERSECUTION OF TRUTH.

They have said among themselves: We will destroy Good, we will smother its germ, even in the depths of souls. And if any one soever dare raise his voice to defend it, to recall to man the memory of it, we will incarcerate him in our dungeons like a criminal, for we have the power, or we will unchain upon him the famished pack which guard the portals of the temple of Evil, which, for the morsel of bread, thrown before them in the dirt, vomit outrage and falsehood.

Fools! and should you do to-day, what death will do to-morrow, would you have thereby conquered? The Good, is it man? I am the Good, says the Lord God.

When the Just One, nailed to the cross, expired between two thieves, the powerful of that time, the politicians, the hypocrites, those who devoured the people, as one devours a piece of bread, believed it a triumph. The following day, the echoes, from one extremity of the earth to the other, sent back a cry of salvation, issuing from the tomb of the Crucified One.

XXXIX.

THE RIGHTS OF THE PEOPLE AND WHAT HAS BECOME OF THEM.

TELL me, oh People! what has become of thy right in this world? tell me what thy wretched life, so overcharged with labor, was in the days of old, and still is?

Slave in former times, afterward serf during long

centuries, always oppressed, preyed upon always, like unto the meadow which is cropped in spring, and left a prey to another ravenous tooth in autumn, what benefit hast thou reaped from what has mockingly been called thy ENFRANCHISEMENT?

Wherefore draggest thou thyself along with so much pain over this earth, devised to all men in common, and over which all should have dominion?

Wherefore in the midst of productions, which it offers spontaneously, and which thy labor multiplies, dost thou so often groan in the anguish of hunger?

Wherefore hast thou no shelter, neither against the frozen blasts of winter, nor against the scorching heat of the sun in summer?

Wherefore wantest thou clothing to cover thy emaciated limbs, and a shroud to inwrap them, when they are thrown into the Potter's field, to rest for the first time?

When the rain falls from the clouds, it refreshes and revives the humblest plant, hidden in the corner of the valley, as well as the tree on the mountain-top, which raises its stately head toward heaven, and stretches forth its powerful branches in defiance to the storm.

Wherefore, uneasy about to-day, and anxious

about to-morrow, do the domestic joys turn for thee into bitter cares? At the table, where it is the will of the common Father that all His children should sit down, why is thy cup never filled but with muddy wine?

From tenderest infancy, absorbed in manual labor, at the cost of how much sacrifice, dost thou reap even a few feeble rays of the light which nourishes the mind? Why does not the star of science appear above the horizon of the gloomy world, whither thou art banished?

Our life on earth, undoubtedly, cannot be exempt from pain. Want, suffering even, as they stimulate our activity, are a condition of the common progress. Without question too, although equals in right, all men do not possess equal faculties, are not all born under circumstances equally favorable to the development of those faculties, and that inequality (whence result, with different inclinations, particular aptitudes for the various functions, implied by the existence of society) contributes to the general welfare.

But in that welfare, all must have a share, and we could not even call it the general welfare, if it were not the well-being of the greater number, the well-being of the people, and not of a few individuals, or of a few classes only. In fact, if one man rolled in riches, all the others remaining poor, would you call his wealth the GENERAL wealth?

Now, almost universally, the possession of the blessings, destined by nature to all, has been the exclusive allotment of a few, who holding the people under their subjection, and forgetful of the sentiment which brother owes to brother, have treated them like animals, which during the day are put to the plough, and into whose stable at night is thrown a handful of straw.

But you should know and well consider this:—When the excess of suffering inspires you with the resolution to recover the rights of which your oppressors have robbed you, you are accused of disturbing the order and treated like rebels. Rebels against whom? There is no rebellion possible but against the real sovereign, against the people, and how is it possible that the people should rebel against themselves? The rebels are those who create themselves iniquitous privileges at their expense; those who, either by craft or strength, succeed in subjecting them to their domination; and when the people shake off that domination, they do not disturb the order, but re-establish it, and accomplish the work of God and His will, which is always just.

XL.

THE LEGACY TO OUR CHILDREN.

You need much patience and a courage which grows not weary: for you will not conquer in a day.

Liberty is the bread which the people must earn in the sweat of their brow.

Many start with ardor, and then become disheartened, before having reached the time of the harvest.

They are like those men, weak and indolent, who not being able to endure the toil of clearing from their fields the weeds from time to time, as they grow, sow and do not reap, because they have suffered the good seed to be choked.

I say unto you, there is always great want in that country.

Again, they are like those foolish men who, having builded as far as the top a home in which to dwell, neglect to roof it, because they are afraid of a little more fatigue.

The winds and the rains come, and the house falls,

and those who had erected it, are suddenly buried beneath its ruins.

If even your expectations may have been disappointed not only seven times, but seventy times seven, never lose hope.

When a man has faith in it, the just cause always triumphs, and that man succeeds who perseveres even to the end.

Say not: The suffering is too great for blessings which will come only late.

If those blessings come late, if you enjoy them but a short time, or even if it be not given unto you to enjoy them at all, your children will enjoy them, and your children's children.

They will have only what you bequeath them: consider then whether you wish to leave them scourges and chains, and hunger for a heritage.

He who asks himself: of what value is justice? defiles justice in his heart; and he who calculates the price of liberty, renounces liberty in his heart.

Liberty and justice will weigh you in the same balance, wherein you shall weigh them. Learn then to understand their worth.

There are nations who have known it not, and no wretchedness ever equalled their wretchedness.

If there is on earth anything sublime, it is the firm resolution of a people who march, under the eye of God, without growing weary an instant, to the conquest of the rights which they hold from Him; who number neither their wounds, nor their days without rest, nor their nights without sleep, and who to themselves say: Of what account are these? Justice and liberty are well worth greater toil.

That people may suffer misfortunes, reverses, treachery, they may be sold by some Judas. Let nothing dishearten them.

For, verily, I say unto you, even should they descend like Christ into the tomb, they like Christ would arise on the third day, conquerors of death, and of the Prince of the world, and of the ministers of the Prince of the world.

XLI.

LIBERTY AND JUSTICE.

The ploughman bears the burden of the day, exposes himself to the rain, to the sun, to the winds, to make ready by his labor for the harvest, which will fill his granaries in autumn.

Justice is the harvest of nations.

The artisan arises before the break of day, lights his small lamp, and toils without ceasing to earn the morsel of bread which sustains him and his children.

Justice is the bread of nations.

The merchant hesitates at no labor, complains of no fatigue; he wastes his body and forgets his sleep, in amassing wealth.

Liberty is the wealth of nations.

The sailor ploughs the seas, risks himself on the waves and in tempests, hazards himself amid shoals, endures cold and heat, to secure for himself some repose in his old age.

Liberty is the repose of nations.

The soldier submits to most cruel privations, he keeps watch and fights, and sheds his blood for what he calls glory.

Liberty is the glory of nations.

If there is a nation which esteems justice and liberty less, than the ploughman his harvest, the artisan his morsel of bread, the merchant his wealth, the sailor his repose and the soldier his glory; raise around that nation a high wall, that its breath may not infect the rest of the earth.

When shall come to the nations the great day of

their judgment, unto it will be said: What hast thou done with thy soul? no sign nor trace of it has been discovered. The pleasures of the brute only have been thine. Thou hast loved the mire, go, wallow in it.

And, on the contrary, the nation which, above all material benefits, shall have given place in its heart to the true blessings; which, to attain them, shall have spared no toil, no fatigue, no sacrifice, will hear these words:

To those who have a soul, be the soul's recompense. Because thou hast loved, beyond all things, liberty and justice, come and enjoy forever justice and liberty.

XLII.

THE SLAVE AND THE FREEMAN.

Thinkest thou that the ox which is fed in the stall to labor under the yoke, and which is fattened for the shambles, is more to be envied than the bull that seeks in freedom his food in the forest?

Thinkest thou that the horse which is saddled and bridled, and which has always plenty of hay in his rack, enjoys a lot, preferable to that of the stallion who, freed from all restraint, neighs and bounds over the plain?

Thinkest thou that the fowl, to which is flung grain in the poultry-yard, is more happy than the wood-pigeon which at morn knows not where it shall find its food for the day?

Thinkest thou that he who saunters at leisure through one of those parks which are called empires, leads a life more sweet than the exile who, from forest to forest and from range to mountain-range, sets out with his heart full of hope to create a fatherland?

Thinkest thou that the stupid serf, sitting at the table of his lord, relishes the exquisite dishes better, than the soldier of liberty his crust of bread?

Thinkest thou that he who falls asleep with the slave's collar around his neck, upon the straw which his master has thrown down for him, enjoys sweeter sleep than he who, after having fought during the day to free himself from every master, rests a few hours at night, on the earth, in the corner of an open field?

Thinkest thou that the poltroon, who everywhere trails the chain of slavery, is less burdened than the man of courage who bears the shackles of the prisoner?

Thinkest thou that the timid man who expires in his bed, suffocated by the impure air which surrounds tyranny, dies a death more desirable than the undaunted man who, upon the scaffold, renders to God a soul, free, as he received it from Him?

Labor is everywhere and suffering everywhere: yet, there are barren labors and fruitful labors, infamous sufferings and glorious sufferings.

XLIII.

THE TWO IDOLS.

If the oppressors of nations were abandoned to themselves, without support, without assistance from others, what could they accomplish against them?

If, to keep them in servitude, they had no other aid but from those who profit by servitude, what would that petty number be, opposed to whole nations?

And this is the wisdom of God, who has so disposed things, that men may always be able to resist tyranny; and tyranny would be impossible, if men understood the wisdom of God.

But having turned their heart to other thoughts,

the rulers of the world have opposed to the wisdom of God, which men understood not, the wisdom of the Prince of the world, Satan.

Now Satan, who is king of the oppressors of nations, suggested to them an infernal scheme, to confirm their tyranny.

He said to them: This is what you should do. Take from each family the young men most robust, and give arms to them, and instruct them in their use, and they will fight for you against their fathers and their brothers; for I will persuade them that it is a glorious deed.

I will make for them two idols, which shall be named Honor and Loyalty, and a law which shall be called passive Obedience.

And they shall worship those idols, and they shall blindly submit to that law, because I will delude their spirit, and you will have no more to fear.

And the oppressors of nations did what Satan had advised, and Satan also accomplished what he had promised to the oppressors of nations.

And the children of the people were seen to lift up their arm against the people, slaughter their brothers, bind in chains their fathers, and forget even the mothers who had borne them.

When it was said to them: In the name of all that is sacred, think of the injustice, of the atrocity of what you are ordered to do, they replied: We do not think, we obey.

And when it was said to them: Is there no longer within you any love for your fathers, your mothers, your brothers and your sisters? they replied: We do not love, we obey.

And when they were shown the altars of the God who created man, and of Christ who saved him, they exclaimed: Those are the Gods of the country; the Gods whom we acknowledge, are the Gods of her rulers, Loyalty and Honor.

Verily, I say unto you, since the beguiling of the first woman by the Serpent, there has been no leading astray more terrible than that.

But the end approaches. When the evil spirit bewitches upright souls, it is but for a time. They pass as it were through a hideous dream, and at their awakening, they bless God who has freed them from that torture.

A few days more, and those who fought for the oppressors, will battle for the oppressed; those who fought to retain in chains their fathers, their mothers, their brothers and their sisters, will battle to set them free.

And Satan will flee to his caverns with the rulers of nations.

XLIV.

NOTHING WITHOUT GOD.

Why do you fatigue yourselves to no purpose in your wretchedness? Your desire is good, but you know not how to accomplish it.

Remember well this maxim: He alone is able to restore life, who has bestowed life.

Without God, you will thrive in nothing.

You writhe upon your bed of anguish: what relief have you found?

You have overthrown a few tyrants, and others have arisen, worse than the first.

You have abolished laws of servitude, and you have had laws of blood, and then laws of servitude again.

Distrust therefore those who interpose between God and you, so that their shadow conceals Him from you. Those men have evil designs.

For from God emanates the power which gives freedom, because from God comes the love which gives union.

For you what can a man do, who has for a rule

but his own thought, and for a law his own will?

Even if he is sincere and wishes only your good, he is compelled to give you his will for a law, and his thought for a rule.

Now, all tyrants do this.

It avails not to overthrow all things, and to expose one's self to all things, in order to substitute for one tyranny another tyranny.

Liberty does not consist in the domination of this one instead of that one, but in the domination of no one.

Now, where God reigns not, it is necessary for a man to rule, and that has always been so.

The reign of God, I say it to you again, is the reign of justice in the mind and of fraternity in the heart: and its foundation on earth is faith in God and faith in Christ, who has proclaimed the law of God, the law of fraternity and the law of justice.

The law of justice teaches that all are equal before their father, who is God, and before their only master, who is Christ.

The law of fraternity tells them to love one another and give mutual aid like sons of the same father and disciples of the same master.

And then they are free, because no one reigns over others, unless he has been chosen voluntarily by all to rule: and their liberty cannot be torn from them, because they are all united for its defense.

But those who say unto you: Prior to us, no one understood what justice was: justice proceeds not from God, it comes from man: entrust yourselves to us, and we will give you justice which will satisfy you.

Such persons delude you, or, if they promise you liberty in sincerity, they deceive themselves.

For they ask you to recognize them for masters, and thus your liberty would be only obedience to these new masters.

Tell them that your master is Christ, that you wish for no other, and Christ will set you free.

XLV.

OBSERVATION OF DUTY—THE FULFILMENT OF THE LAW.

Duty extends itself to all beings, for all have their place in the Universe; all—according to the views of Supreme Wisdom—fulfil functions, which it is forbidden to disturb; all enjoy the gift divine, and have a right to enjoy it. To destroy a single one among them from pure caprice, or inflict upon him useless sufferings, is a wicked action, an action, opposed to the laws of order.

Respect God in His least works, and that your love, like His, embrace everything that breathes and lives.

If, in endowing man with intellect, He has made him the king of nature, His will was not that man should be the tyrant of nature. His eye, from which nothing escapes, has a fatherly care also for the poor sparrow, which quivers with fear under your hand.

No society is possible without duty, for without it, there can exist no tie among men.

Interrogate everywhere unprejudiced reason, and the conscience which neither self-interest nor passion has corrupted, and they will answer you: that man is sacred to man; that to attack him in his person, in his liberty or in his property, is to overthrow the basis of order, is to violate the moral, preservative laws of mankind, is to perpetrate one of those acts, which in all centuries and among all nations have received the terrible name of CRIME.

There exists a voice without you, immutable, eternal, and another voice within you; and both those voices tell you:

Thou shalt do no murder; thou shalt not steal; thou shalt dishonor neither the virtue of the wife, nor the chastity of the young maiden; thy thought even shall be clean of those abominations.

Whosoever spills the blood of his brother, is accursed on earth and accursed in Heaven.

And accursed also is he, who through craft or violence, takes away from his brother either his liberty, or what portion soever of that which he possesses legitimately; who carries into his family disorder, with all the evils to which disorder gives birth: shame, discord, the torments of mind, distrust, hatred and oftentimes ruin.

The plants of the fields, grouped together, extend their roots in the soil, which nourishes them all, and all grow up in peace. Not one of them absorbs the sap of another, causes its blossom to wither, or spoils its fragrance. Wherefore is man less kind to man?

Banish from your heart all wicked desires and all wicked thoughts; for to take a delight in the thought and in the desire of evil, is already to have accomplished the evil.

There are words which kill; be watchful therefore over your tongue, and that it never be soiled with evil-speaking and slander.

Envy, anger, vindictiveness, hatred, devour the soul which conceals them, and that tormented soul is perpetually as if in travail to give birth to murder.

Have you been offended? forgive, that you may be forgiven. Who does not stand in need of forgiveness? and who can say to himself: not one could with justice complain of me?

Do not walk in tortuous paths, and let your word be always true; that it never offend the ear of chastity, nor wound the respect which man owes to man, and owes to himself.

He also owes to himself that he should shun everything which would degrade and debase him, by bringing him nearer to the brute: all the excesses of the senses, fatal habits which wear out the body, stupefy the mind, and make beholders, no longer recognizing in him an intelligent creature, turn aside their eyes from him with disgust.

In us there exist two beings, the animal and the angel, and our labor should be to combat the one, in order that the other dominate alone, until the moment, when liberated from his weighty envelope, he shall take his flight towards better and higher regions.

Acting in this manner, you will injure no one, you will be just; but other duties besides, grand and sacred duties will remain for you to fulfill.

Has he, who has simply refrained from evil, who has done to his fellow-creature neither the slightest wrong, nor the slightest good, has he fulfilled his duties to him, and is he perfect before God? In depositing at the bottom of our heart the germ of love and of pity, of all sympathetic feeling, has not the Father in heaven commanded us other virtues, more elevated and more far-reaching?

Behold yonder poor human creature, lying at the corner of the street, fainting from want, or whom an accident has cast mangled there. A man looks at him, pities him and passes by. Am I the cause, says he to himself, that he is there in that condition, and who has made me his keeper? It is more than enough that one must think of one's self. Another looks upon him also, and his heart is moved. He approaches, takes him in his arms, carries him to his home, lays him on his bed, watches by him, and takes care of him as a brother takes care of a brother, and a friend of his friend.

Which of these two men has truly accomplished his duty?

There will always be evils on earth, and those evils must always be remedied.

Is your brother hungry: you owe him the nourishment he is in want of; is he naked, without roof, without refuge: you owe him clothing and a place of shelter; sick, you owe him assistance. He is your flesh, for you are all members of one and the same body, which one and the same soul must animate: treat him therefore as your own flesh.

There are many kinds of weakness and many sorts of destitution; and each weakness has a claim to protection, every destitution to relief. But for that, I ask you, what would be human society? what would be the world? What would become of those whom infirmity, poverty, isolation, old age, simplicity of mind and ignorance leave an easy prey to the snares of the wicked?

Resent the injustice, done unto others, with the same energy, the same resolution, as if it were done unto yourself; stretch forth your hand between the oppressor and the oppressed. Your brother is yourself, and if he is oppressed, are you not oppressed likewise?

Let the orphan find in you a father; the widow and the old man a staff of support; the stranger a helpful host; be the eye of the blind man, and the foot of the cripple.

To the afflicted speak those words from the heart, which soothe the bitterness of their tears. There are no sufferings which sympathy does not alleviate. The sorrows of life are dissipated by the rays of fraternal love, even as the frosts in autumn melt away before the morning-sun.

Whoever gives in season good advice, a wise warning, or useful instruction, gives more than if he gave gold; and to impart that which one knows, to spread science, is sowing the seed which will nourish successive generations.

Do not think that you can do too much, in order to obtain peace: peace, which is the foundation of all happiness, is at the same time its crowning-work. Bear with others, that they may bear with you. Have we not all our foibles, our failings, our disagreeable moments? patience gradually softens the rudest asperities; let nothing then exhaust your patience, neither irritating words, nor provoking levity. Be like unto the vine, whose juice is so much the sweeter, as it grows in a stonier soil.

To respect the life, the liberty, and the property of others;

To assist others in the preserving and the developing of their life, their liberty, and their property;

These two precepts contain in substance the duties of justice and fraternity. To detail them, would be infinite, for they include all the thoughts, all the feelings, all the actions of man, and one single precept comprises them all, the divine precept of love. Love, and do whatever you please, for you shall wish for nothing but what is just and good. Love, says the sovereign Master, and thou shalt perfectly fulfil the law.

XLVI.

THE PROPHET.

When fraternity had frozen up, and injustice had commenced to flourish on the earth, God spoke to one of His servants: Go unto that people from me, and proclaim to them what thou shalt see; and that which thou shalt see, will surely come to pass, unless, quitting their evil ways, they repent and return unto me.

And the servant of God obeyed His command, and having clad himself in sackcloth, and having sprinkled ashes upon his head, he went to that multitude, and raising his voice, said:

Wherefore do you kindle the anger of the Lord to your own destruction? Quit your evil ways: repent and return unto Him.

And some, hearing these words, were moved, and others scoffed, saying: Who is he, and what comes he to tell us? Who has given him the right to reprimand us? He is a fool.

And behold, the Spirit of God came upon the prophet, and time was opened to his eyes, and the centuries passed before him.

And suddenly rending his clothes: Thus, said he, will be dismembered the race of Adam.

The men of iniquity have measured the earth with a cord: they have numbered its inhabitants, as one numbers cattle, head by head.

They have said: Let us divide this among ourselves, and let us make it valuable for our use.

And the division has been made; and each has taken what fell to his lot, and the earth and its inhabitants have become the possession of the men of iniquity, and consulting together, they have asked one another: What is our possession worth? and together they have answered: Thirty pieces of silver.

And they have commenced to traffic among themselves with those thirty pieces of silver.

There have been purchases, sales, exchanges; men for land, land for men, and the balance in gold.

And each has coveted the share of the other, and they have begun to butcher one another for the purpose of mutually despoiling one another, and, in the blood which flowed, they have written upon a slip of paper: Right, and upon another: Glory.

Oh Lord! enough, enough!

There are two who cast their hooks of iron upon a nation. Each bears away his fragment.

The sword is sharpened and sharpened again. Do you hear those heart-rending cries? they are the plaints of young wives and the wailings of mothers.

Two spectres glide through the shadows; they haste over the plains and through the cities. The one, fleshless as a skeleton, gnaws at the remains of an unclean beast; the other has in his arm-pit a black fester, and the jackals follow him howling.

Lord, Lord, shall Thy wrath be everlasting? Shall

Thine arm never stretch forth but to strike? Spare the fathers for the sake of the children. Suffer Thyself to be moved by the tears of those poor little creatures, who are not yet able to distinguish their left hand from their right.

The world grows broader, peace will be born again, there will be room for all.

Woe! woe! blood flows on: it encircles the earth like a girdle of red.

Who is that aged man, who talks of justice, holding in one hand a cup of poison, and caressing with the other a prostitute, who calls him father?

He says: To me belongs the race of Adam. Among you, who are the strongest? I will distribute that race!

And what he has said, he does, and from his throne, without rising, he assigns to each his prey.

And all gorge, gorge; and their hunger grows more clamorous, and they rush upon one another, and the flesh quivers, and the bones crack in their teeth.

A market-place is opened, the nations are driven there with a cord around their neck; their muscles are felt, they are weighed, they are made to run and to walk: they are valued at so much. It is no longer the former tumult and confusion, it is commerce regularly conducted.

Happy the birds of the air and the animals of the earth! no one restrains them, they go and come as they please.

What are those mill-stones which turn without ceasing, and what do they grind?

Children of Adam, those mill-stones are the laws of those who rule you, and you are the grist which they grind.

And in proportion as the prophet cast upon the future these ill-boding gleams, a strange terror seized upon those who listened.

Suddenly his voice ceased to be heard, and he seemed as if absorbed in profound thought. The people waited in silence, their heart oppressed and beating with anguish.

Then the prophet: Lord, Thou hast not abandoned this people in its misery; Thou hast not delivered it for ever to its oppressors.

And he took two twigs, and he stripped off their leaves, and crossing them, he bound them together, and raised them on high over the multitude, saying: This shall be your salvation; you shall conquer by this emblem.

And night came on, and the prophet disappeared as a shadow which passes, and the multitude dispersed on all sides in the darkness.

XLVII.

THE CONSPIRACY OF EVIL.

Satan, one day, assembled his minions, and said to them: It is vain to tempt men in a thousand ways, to push them upon the decline, where they slide so rapidly, our work advances little; what we gain on the one hand, we lose on the other. Why is this?

Each of the infernal powers extolling himself, accused the others, until wrath and hatred being kindled, nothing was longer heard but jarring sounds, yells of anger, the hiss of burning breath, mingled with words of phrensy, of threat, and of blasphemy. In the black pit a horrible conflict was impending, when the king of the fallen legions suddenly drawing himself to his full height, sent forth his voice, formidable and awful as subterranean thunder.

Silence! it said; and there was silence.

That which ye know not, continued Satan, I

know. Our efforts have been in part futile, because ill-concerted, they lacked unison. Each of you, according to his fancy, has sown here and there at random, without calculation and without foresight, and this is why at harvest-time we have gathered ears and not sheaves.

Should this continue, as well might I yield up my empire. Think ye that Satan will so resolve? No! to all eternity, no!

I will raise the city of evil, I will lay its foundation upon this earth which a rival power contests with me.

For that audacity is without doubt necessary; but there is necessity also for prudence. Let us hasten nothing. Let a centre first be established, from which our action shall spring, from which it shall flow stream upon stream and insinuate itself, by a thousand various ways, even to the extremities of that great body, called society. Let us breathe into its heart the fire with which we burn, that it may unknowingly consume them.

Fierce acclamations greeted these words of Satan.

And the earth, seized with sudden fear, trembled; and the sun was veiled, and the air became dark; from the grave-yards arose slowly vapors, dense, livid, grey and reddish, and in the distance was heard a tolling like funeral-bells.

And in the slums of a great city, in as it were a sink, whence exhaled an odor of corruption, I saw a crowd to which I can give no name. Their horrid faces had the features of man, but not the expression. Their retreating brows, their ghastly cheeks, here and there streaked with red, or marked with purple spots, wore the hideous stamp of base crime and brutish vice. There could be read in their eyes glowing or glassy, in their sneaking gaze, all the nature of the beast of prey, of vile wickedness, cunning, craft, something of the serpent, something also of the hyena.

There were of all kinds and of all aspects, from the beggar clothed in rags to him who displays on splendid robes the prostituted emblems of a false glory and infamous honor.

From a high-raised seat, one of them, surrounded by inferior chiefs, inured to the hardships of hell, gave to the crowd his orders. He divided them into two bands. The one was to show itself in broad day, the other to creep unseen through the public places and even into the privacy, everywhere sacred, of the domestic hearth; and they were commanded to act together, each to support and aid the other.

Something, I know not what, revolting as the sneer of evil, curled the lips of him who was surrounded in silence by all these human spectres.

To those, appointed to skulk in the shadows, he said:

These shall be your gods: falsehood, perjury, hypocrisy, corruption. You shall spread everywhere suspicion, jealousies. At times also, you shall lull to sleep credulous simplicity, that your purposes may the better be served. You shall beguile and you shall betray. You shall search hearts, that you may discover the germs of vice, which may there be concealed, and, at the agreed price, you shall furnish to each his demands. Proceed artfully, allure, seduce, veiling the consequences, until return is no longer possible. And want also, extreme want, shall be for you a powerful instrument. You shall say to famine: Sell me this one, that one, and if there is hesitation, you shall point out to the father the yawning tomb which awaits his wife, his children, and you shall ring in his ear their cries of anguish. You shall spread your snares for the step of the unsuspecting man, you shall suggest to him things concerning which he had not the least thought, you shall urge him upon perilous paths, and if not successful, understand this well, you shall create that which is not. Go. And he flung to them pieces of gold, upon which they threw themselves with avidity.

To the others he said:

As for you, your gods shall be violence and menace. You shall threaten the feeble, the poor, you shall make him desolate by your persecutions, you shall snatch from him the crust of bread soaked in his sweat, if he do not blindly comply with all that you require of him.

Let all obey with the dumb docility of the beast of burden. Let them think as we do, or not think at all, or let them bear the penalty of thought in rebellion.

I have chosen you for a work, conforming to your nature. You shall have your banquets, where shall be tears, wounds, blood, blood which shall flow without danger to you, without resistance to you, for such is our courage.

Having said this, all dispersed, and the great city was like a tree, at whose foot has been poured out fluid poison, which is absorbed through the roots, and which, mounting with the sap, withers the blossoms, the fruit, the leaves, and rots the dead branches.

And it seemed to me that I was the victim of a horrible dream, when suddenly a confused noise woke me from my stupor. It was voices of anger, blended with snappings as of broken limbs, heart-rending groans and savage laughter, and I beheld a multitude of young men, of children, mangled, blood-stained, who were crowded and heaped in the sink, whence the drunken lands of the spirit of Satan had issued, and the iron-bound gates opened and closed of themselves, awful was the silence.

And I was transported to a dim hall. I recognized him who ruled in that place; he was not alone: near him pressed and thronged dark phantoms, with whom he counseled in a low tone.

And after a short time, the dark phantoms withdrew. I wished to follow them, but they disappeared in passages, gloomy and winding, where the poisoned air suffocated me.

As I, overwhelmed with sadness and filled with terror, was considering these things, lo! the same crowd, which I had seen thrust into the sink, reappears to my eyes, always displaying the same ghastly looks. They drove them forward, through a doorway, narrow and low, into a sort of cavern, where I perceived scowling faces, such as are seen on the scaffold, around the doomed criminal, and I heard sounds, shrill and hoarse, and savage jests, and terrible curses, and I felt myself plunged into a dense vapor of fetid odor, like that which rises from the tomb, and I nearly swooned.

And those who had been cast there grew pale hour by hour, and feeble, and bent. The air refused to enter their panting breast, and their bones rattled together like the bones of a skeleton, and in the morning was seen, without mourners, without prayers, carried away in silence some fleeting coffin.

And from my soul, filled with unspeakable agony, this cry escaped:

Lord, can Satan have been the victor?

And a voice said to me: Behold!

And I raised my eyes, and saw in the divine light the martyrs who smiled.

XLVIII.

THE AGED MAN AND THE PILGRIM.

In the time when the leaves grow yellow, an aged man, loaded with a bundle of twigs, returned slowly to his hut, situated on the declivity of a vale.

And at the opening of the vale, between a few trees, scattered here and there, were seen the oblique rays of the sun, already descended below the horizon, sporting on the clouds of the west, and tinging them with numberless hues, which faded away little by little.

And the aged man, having arrived at his hut, his only wealth, together with the small piece of ground near by, which he cultivated, cast down his bundle of twigs, seated himself upon a wooden bench, black with smoke from the hearth, and dropped his head upon his breast in profound reverie.

And from time to time his overcharged breast allowed a convulsive sob to escape, and in a cracked voice, he said:

I had but one son, they have taken him from me; but one poor cow, they have taken her from me for the tax of my little field.

And then, with a voice more feeble, he repeated: My son, my son; and a teardrop moistened his aged lashes, but it could not fall.

As he was thus grieving, he heard some one who said: Father, may the blessing of God rest upon you and yours!

Mine, said the aged man, I have no longer one to call mine; I am alone.

And raising his eyes, he beheld a pilgrim, standing at the door, resting upon a long staff; and knowing that the guest is sent of God, he said to him:

May God requite your benediction! Come in, my son: what the poor hath, belongs to the poor.

And kindling upon the hearth his bundle of twigs, he began to make ready a repast for the traveler.

But nothing was able to divert the thought which oppressed him: it rested constantly upon his heart.

And the pilgrim, having learned what so sorely distressed him, said: Father, God tries you at the hand of men. Yet, there are calamities greater than yours. It is not the oppressed that suffer most, it is the oppressor.

The aged man shook his head, and answered not.

The pilgrim continued: What you now believe not, you shortly will believe.

And having caused him to sit down, with his hands he touched his eyes, and the aged man sunk into a slumber, heavy, dark and full of horrors, as was the slumber which fell upon Abraham, when God showed to him the coming misfortunes of his race.

And it seemed to him as if he were transported to a vast palace, beside a couch; near by the couch was a crown, and on the couch a sleeping man, whose thoughts the aged man could read as clearly as, awake by day, we see that which passes before our eyes.

And the man lying there, stretched upon the couch of gold, seemed to hear the confused cries of a multitude, asking for bread. It was a sound like the roar of the surge which breaks against the shore in the storm. And the tempest grew more violent; and the roar increased; and the man who slept, saw the waves moment by moment rise higher and still more high, and beat even against the walls of the palace, and he made most terrible efforts to flee, but could not, and his agony was extreme.

Whilst he gazed in terror, the aged man was suddenly transported to another palace. He who lay stretched out there, rather resembled a corpse than one living.

And in his sleep, he beheld before him severed heads; and opening their mouths, those heads said:

We had devoted ourselves to thee, and this is the reward which we have received. Sleep on, sleep on, we sleep not. We await the hour of vengeance: it approaches.

And the blood curdled in the veins of the sleeper. And to himself he said: If I might at least leave my crown to this child: and his haggard eyes turned upon a cradle, on which was placed a queen's diadem.

But when he grew more tranquil, and drew a little comfort from this thought, another, resembling him in feature, seized the child and crushed it against the wall.

And the aged man felt himself swooning with horror.

And he was transported at the same moment into two different places; and although far separated, the places to him seemed but one.

And he beheld two men who, but for their age, might have been mistaken the one for the other, and he knew that they had been borne by the same mother.

And their sleep was that of the condemned to be

executed at his wakening. Shapes, wrapped in bloody shrouds, passed before them, and each, in passing by, touched them, and their limbs quivered and contracted as if to escape that deathly touch.

Then they gazed upon each other with something like a hideous smile, and their eyes flashed fire, and their hand moved convulsively to the handle of a dagger.

And the aged man next saw a man, wan and emaciated. Suspicion glided in multitudes by his bed, distilled their venom upon his face, whispered in a low tone sinister words, and slowly sunk their claws into his skull, which was moist with cold perspiration. And a human form, white as a winding-sheet, approached him, and without speaking, pointed with its finger to a livid spot which it had around its neck. And in the bed where he lay, the knees of the pale man rattled together, and his mouth fell open in terror, and his eyes dilated with fear.

And the aged man, benumbed with fright, was transported to a palace more vast.

And he who slumbered there, breathed only with the greatest difficulty. A black spectre was squatted upon his breast and grinned at him. And it chattered in his ear, and its words became visions to the mind of the man whom it pressed down and lacerated with its sharp bones.

And he saw himself surrounded with a numberless multitude, who rent the air with fearful cries:

Thou hast promised us liberty, and thou hast given us servitude.

Thou hast promised us to reign by law, and the laws are thy mere caprices.

Thou hast promised that thou wouldst spare the bread of our wives and of our children, and thou hast doubled our burdens to swell thine own treasures.

Thou hast promised us glory, and hast given us up to the scorn of nations and their just hatred.

Descend, descend, and sleep with perjurers and tyrants.

And he felt himself hurled down, dragged by that multitude, and he clung to his sacks of gold, and the sacks burst, and the gold scattered and fell to the earth.

And it seemed to him as if he wandered forlorn through the world, and, thirsty, asked for a drink in charity, and that a glass of dregs was offered him, and that all shunned him, all cursed him, because his brow was branded with the mark of traitor.

And the aged man in disgust turned away his eyes.

And in two other palaces, he saw two other men, dreaming of executions. For, said they, where shall we find security? The ground is sapped beneath our feet; the nations abhor us; the little children even, in their prayers, ask God, night and morn, that the earth may be delivered from us.

And the one condemned to HARSH IMPRISONMENT, that is to say to all the tortures of body and soul, and to death by hunger, the wretches whom he suspected of having uttered the word fatherland; and the other, after having seized upon their property, ordered to be thrown into the depths of a dungeon two young maidens, guilty of having cared for their wounded brothers in a hospital.

And as they grew weary in the labor of execution, messengers came to them.

And one of the messengers said: Your southern provinces have burst their chains, and with the links they have driven away your rulers and your soldiers.

And the other: your eagles have been plucked on the banks of the great river: its waves bear away the debris.

And the two kings writhed upon their couch.

And the aged man saw a third. He had banished God from his heart, and in his heart, in place of God, was a worm which gnawed him incessantly; and when the torture became more intense, he muttered indistinct blasphemies, and his lips were covered with bloody froth.

And he seemed to be in an immense plain, alone with the worm which left him not. And that plain was a grave-yard, the grave-yard of a slaughtered people.

And behold, suddenly the earth trembles; the tombs burst open, the dead arise and advance in crowds: and he could neither move, nor cry out.

And all those dead, men, women, children, gazed upon him in silence: and after a short time, in the same silence, they raised the stones from the tombs, and placed them around him.

First he was walled up to his knee, then to his breast, then to his mouth, and with a powerful effort he strained the muscles of his neck to breathe once more; and the wall continually grew higher, and when it was finished, its top was lost in a dark cloud.

The strength of the aged man began to leave him; his soul was overcome with terror.

And behold, having traversed several deserted halls, in a small chamber, on a bed, dimly lightened by a feeble lamp, he sees a man worn with age.

Around the bed were seven terrors, four on one side, three on the other.

And one of the terrors laid his hand upon the heart of the decrepit man, and he trembled, and his limbs shook; and the hand rested there as long as it felt any heat.

And after this one, another more cold did as the first, and all laid their hand upon the heart of the decrepit man.

And there passed within him things, impossible to unveil.

He beheld in the distance, toward the pole, a hideous phantom, which said to him: Yield thyself up to me, and I will warm thee with my breath.

And with his frozen fingers, the terrified man wrote down a pact, I know not what, but each word was like a death-rattle.

And this was the last vision. And the aged man having awaked, rendered thanks to Providence for the lot which it had given to him in the sufferings of life.

And the pilgrim said to him: Hope and pray; prayer obtains all. Your son is not lost; your eyes shall behold him again before closing. Await in peace the day of God.

And the aged man awaited in peace.

XLIX.

THE MILLENNIUM.

WHEN, after a long drought, a gentle rain falls upon the earth, it drinks up with avidity the water from Heaven, which refreshes it and makes it fertile.

Thus, the thirsting nations will drink in with avidity the word of God, as it descends upon them like a summer-shower.

And justice with love, and peace and liberty will spring up in their breast.

And it will be as in the time when all were brothers, and there will be heard no more the voice of the master, nor the voice of the slave, the groans of the poor, nor the sighs of the oppressed, only songs of gladness and of thanksgiving.

Fathers will say to their sons: Our early days were troubled, full of tears and of anguish. Now the sun rises and sets upon our joy. Praised be God, who has shown us these mercies before death!

And mothers will say to their daughters: Behold our brows, now so smooth; formerly affliction, grief, unrest traced there deep furrows. Yours are like the surface of a lake in spring-time, agitated by no breeze. Praised be God, who has shown us these mercies before death!

And the young men will say to the youthful maidens: You are beautiful as the flowers of the field, pure as the dew which refreshes them, as the light which gives them color. It is sweet to see our fathers, sweet to be near our mothers; but when we behold you and are near you, there moves in our souls something unnamed but in Heaven. Praised be God, who has shown us these mercies before death!

And the youthful maidens will reply: The flowers fade, they pass away; there comes a day, when no more the dew refreshes them, nor the light gives them color. There is upon the earth only virtue, which never fades nor passes away. Our fathers are like the ripened ear in autumn, and our mothers like the vine, loaded with fruit. It is sweet to see our fathers; it is sweet to be at our mothers' side: and the sons of our fathers and of our mothers are also dear to us. Praised be God, who has shown us these mercies before death!

L.

LIFE AND DEATH.

THAT marvelous order, those beautiful and touching harmonies which charm us in nature, whence do they come? From everything being in its place, and maintaining itself there invariably. Each being, obeying with punctual regularity the general laws and its particular laws, faithfully fulfils the function which the Creator assigned to it. From the sun, whence pour forth inexhaustible torrents of light and of life, to the river-source which comes down, drop by drop, from the rock—everything is regulated to one and the same design, and everything contributes to it in an infinite variety of ways, which our thought admires more and more, the longer we contemplate them. There is not in the Universe one action, one movement, which does not, immediately one after another, co-operate in the growth of the moss-plant; and the different worlds, after having gone like the moss-plant through all the phases of development, are decomposed like it: to furnish nourishment for other worlds.

There is not one creature whose existence does not depend upon other creatures. In order that they may subsist, a continual transfusion of their entity must take place. What is life? To receive. What is death? To give. Life, in its first condition, is a sacrifice, a perpetual and universal communion.

That which inert bodies, plants, animals destitute of reason, do blindly and necessarily, subjected as they are to a fatal, irresistible impulse, man must do freely; subordinating himself to the whole, of which he is a member, he must love his brothers as he loves himself, wish for their happiness as he wishes for his own, rejoice in their joys, grieve over their troubles, help them, serve them, identify himself with them, sacrifice himself for them, and in this manner, through an evermore growing union of individuals and nations, work at consummating the Holy Unity of Mankind.

LI.

THE TRUE END OF LIFE.

Wherefore run ye after shadows? Why do you forget your true end?

Deceitful glimmerings, alluring voices invite you to places, barren and desolate, where hope herself dies away in never ending night.

The wants of the flesh, who will deny? must be satisfied; it is the condition of existence. But the wants, is that all? The appetites, is that all?

Are you then body only, that you seek in the body the good, immense, without bounds, to which you aspire?

To-morrow, what will that body be? A handful of ashes. Each day it advances toward the grave. Is that the pathway of your desires?

The brute even buries not itself wholly in its senses and in the enjoyments of sense. It has instincts more elevated, joys more intense. Without knowing, it shows you from afar the goal toward which you should tend.

Do you wish to sink below the brute? and if you so wish, of what do you complain? Does one stoop so low without distress? Can one struggle against his nature, slaughter it without suffering?

That dark spectre, shapeless and without speech, which stifles you in its embrace, know ye its name? Its name is Matter.

Tell them this, for I pity that poor people:

The body is not man, but the covering of man.

Life is not eating and drinking, but intellectual and loving.

The lowest beings of the Creation eat and drink, and that suffices them; man thinks, loves, devotes, gives himself up, that I may give Myself to him, and that he may find in Me, in the True, in the Good, in the Beautiful, the aliment for his soul, that through which he really lives.

What remains? Very little. Seek first My justice, and you shall receive the little in addition.

Woe unto him who wanders in the bottom of the valley, on the borders of the standing waters! The corn, destined to appease your hunger, grows not in the mire: I have sown on the high places the grain which shall nourish you.

LII.

WE WALK IN DARKNESS.

That which thine eyes behold, that which thine hands touch, are mere shadows, and the sound, which strikes thine ear, is but a rough echo of the voice internal and mysterious, which worships, and prays, and groans in the womb of creation.

For every creature is groaning, every creature is in the travail of childbed, and struggling for birth into true life, for passage from darkness to light, from the region of shadows to that of realities.

That sun, so brilliant, so beautiful, is but the garment, the uncertain emblem of the true sun, which illumines and warms the soul.

That earth, so rich, so green, is but the winding-sheet of nature: for nature, fallen into decay also, has gone down to the tomb like man, but like him she will come forth.

In this heavy wrapping of flesh, you resemble a traveler, who at night in his tent sees, or thinks he sees phantoms pass.

The real world is veiled from you. He who retires wholly within himself, catches a glimpse of it as from afar. Secret powers, which slumber in him, awake for a moment, lift a corner of the veil which time holds in his shriveled hand, and the eye turned inward is ravished by the wonders it beholds.

You are sitting on the shore of the ocean of being, but you cannot penetrate its depths. You walk in the evening beside the sea, and you see but a little foam, cast upon the strand by the surge.

With what shall I compare you further?

You are like the child in the womb of its mother, awaiting the hour of birth; like the winged insect in the worm that creeps, eager for the moment to come out from this earthly prison to take wing for Heaven.

LIII.

THE CHURCH-YARD.

At the hour when the East commences to grow dusky, when all sounds die away, he trod slowly, beside the ripening fields, the solitary path.

The bee had returned to its hive, the bird to its nightly perch; the leaves slumbered motionless upon their stems; a sad, sweet silence enwrapped the drowsy earth.

A single voice, the distant voice of the village church-bell, vibrated through the calm air.

It said: Remember the dead.

And, as if fascinated by his dreams, it seemed to him that the voice of the dead, weak and uncertain, mingled with that voice in the air.

Do you return to visit the places where your rapid journey was completed, to seek there souvenirs of griefs and joys which so quickly passed?

Like the smoke, which rises from our thatched roof and suddenly disappears, so you have vanished.

Your tombstones are becoming moss-grown beneath the yew-tree in yonder grave-yard. When the dewy zephyrs whisper in the high grass, one might call it the sighing of spirits. Spouses of death, is it you who tremble upon your mysterious bed?

Now, you are at peace: no more cares, no more tears; now for you shine stars more brilliant; a sun more radiant floods with his splendors plains, ethereal seas and boundless horizons.

Oh, tell me of the mysteries of that world which my longings foreshadow, into the midst of which my soul, wearied by the shadows of earth, yearns to lose itself. Tell me of Him who made it and occupies it, and alone is able to fill the vast emptiness which He has left in me.

Brothers, after waiting, consoled by faith, your hour is come. Mine also will come, and others, in their turn, their day of labor finished, re-entering their wretched huts, will give ear to the voice that says: Remember the dead.

LIV.

THE EXILE.

He went about, wandering over the earth. Be Thou, oh God, the guide of the poor exile!

I have passed among the different nations, and they have looked at me, and I have looked at them, and we have not recognized one another. The exile is everywhere alone.

When, at the decline of day, I saw the smoke arise from a hut in the depth of the valley, I said to myself: Happy the man who, at night, returns to the domestic fireside, and sits down there in the midst of his family. The exile is everywhere alone.

Whither go those clouds, which the storm drives onward? It drives me onward like them, and what do I care whither? The exile is everywhere alone.

These trees are beautiful, these flowers are beautiful; but they are not the flowers and trees of my country: they say nothing to me. The exile is everywhere alone.

This brooklet runs smoothly through the plain; but its purling is not that, to which the ear of my childhood listened: it calls back to my soul not one reminiscence. The exile is everywhere alone.

Those songs are sweet; but the melancholy and the gladness which they awake, are neither my melancholy, nor my gladness. The exile is everywhere alone.

They have asked me: Why do you weep? and when I told them the reason, none has wept with me, because none understood me. The exile is everywhere alone.

I have seen aged men, surrounded with children, like the olive-tree with its shoots; but not one of those aged men called me son, not one of those children called me brother. The exile is everywhere alone.

I have seen young maidens smile with a smile, as pure as the breeze of morning, on him, whom their love had chosen for a spouse; but not one has smiled on me. The exile is everywhere alone.

I have seen young men embrace breast to breast,

as if of two lives they would make but one; but not one has shaken hands with me. The exile is everywhere alone.

There are no friends, no wives, no fathers, no brothers, but in one's native country. The exile is everywhere alone.

Poor exile! cease thy lamentations; all are banished like thyself: all see pass away and vanish fathers, brothers, wives and friends.

Our fatherland is not here below; man seeks it here in vain; what he calls so, is only a resting-place for the night.

He goes about, wandering over the earth. Be Thou, oh God, the guide of the poor exile!

LV.

THE TRINITY.

AND the fatherland was shown unto me.

I was borne away beyond the region of shadows, and I saw time carry them off with indescribable swiftness through the void, as one sees the breeze from the South carry away the light vapors which creep in the distance over the plain.

And I ascended, higher and still more high; and

realities, invisible to the eye of flesh, became visible to me, and in that world of phantoms I heard sounds which have no echo.

And what I heard, what I beheld, was so real, my soul laid hold of it with such vigor, that it seemed to me as if all, I formerly thought I had seen and heard, was but a vague dream of the night.

What shall I declare then unto the children of night, and what are they able to understand? And from the heights of eternal day, am I not also fallen back with them into the bosom of night, into the region of time and of shadows?

I saw, as it were, an ocean, moveless, vast, infinite; and within that ocean, three oceans: an ocean of strength, an ocean of light, an ocean of life; and these three oceans, penetrating one another without mingling, formed but a single ocean, but one unity, indivisible, absolute, eternal.

And that unity was He that is; and in the midst of His being, a wondrous knot bound together three Persons, who were named to me, and their names were the Father, the Son, the Spirit; and there was a generating mysterious, a breathing mysterious, vigorous, fruitful; and the Father, the Son, the Spirit, were He that is.

And the Father appeared to me as a Power which, within the Being Infinite, one with it, has but a single function, lasting, perfect, without limit, which is the Infinite Being Himself.

And the Son appeared to me as a Word, lasting, perfect, without limit, which proclaims the works of the power of the Father, that which He is, that which is the Being Infinite.

And the Spirit appeared to me as the Love, the effusion, the mutual aspiration of the Father and of the Son, animating them with a common life, animating with a life lasting, perfect, without limit, the Infinite Being.

And these three were One, and these three were God, and they embraced one another and were united in the impenetrable sanctuary of the one substance; and that union, that embrace, were, in the bosom of immensity, the eternal joy, the eternal felicity of Him that is.

And in the midst of that infinite ocean of being, creation swum and floated and expanded itself; like an island that should constantly expand its coasts in a sea without shore.

It expanded like a flower which takes root in the water, and extends its long stems and its petals on the surface.

And I beheld the beings link themselves to other beings, and reproduce and develop themselves in their numberless variety, drinking in plentifully, nourishing themselves with a sap which never dries up, with the strength, with the light and with the life of Him that is.

And all that had been hidden from me until then, was unveiled to my gaze, which was no longer obstructed by the material envelope of existence.

Liberated from earthly clogs, I went from world to world, as here below the mind flies from thought to thought; and after having been plunged, lost in those wonders of the Power, of the Wisdom and of the love, I plunged, I lost myself in the very fountain of Love, of Wisdom and of Power.

And I understood what is the fatherland; and I was intoxicated with light, and my soul, enraptured with strains of harmony, sank to sleep on the celestial waves, in an indescribable ecstasy.

And then I beheld Christ on the right hand of His father, radiant with a glory immortal.

And I beheld Him also like a mystic lamb, sacrificed upon an altar; myriads of angels and the men, redeemed by His blood, surrounded Him, and singing His praises, they rendered thanks unto Him in the language of heaven.

And a drop of blood from the Lamb fell upon nature faint and sick, and I saw her transfigured; and all the creatures which she supports, throbbed with new life, and all raised their voice, and that voice said:

Holy, Holy, Holy, is He who hath destroyed evil and conquered death.

And the Son rested in the bosom of the Father, and the Spirit overspread them with His shadow, and there was among them a mystery divine, and the heavens in silence trembled.

THE DEAD.

They also have passed over this earth; they have descended the river of time; their voice was heard on its banks, and then was heard no more. Where are they? Who can tell us? *Happy the dead who die in the Lord!*

Whilst they were passing, a thousand vain shadows presented themselves to their eyes; the world which Christ has accursed, displayed to them its grandeurs, its riches, its pleasures; they beheld it, and suddenly they beheld nothing but eternity. Where are they? Who can tell us? *Happy the dead who die in the Lord!*

Like a ray from on high, a cross, in the distance, appeared to guide their course: but all did not look upon it. Where are they? Who can tell us? *Happy the dead who die in the Lord!*

Some among them said: What mean these waves which bear us away? Is there anything after this rapid voyage? We know not, no one knows. And as they said this, the banks vanished. Where are they? Who can tell us? *Happy the dead who die in the Lord!*

Some also, in deep meditation, seemed to listen to mysterious words; and then, with eye fixed on the west, they suddenly sang to an invisible aurora and a day which never ends. Where are they? Who can tell us? *Happy the dead who die in the Lord!*

Carried away without distinction, young and old, all disappeared as the ship, which the tempest drives onward. It would be easier to count the sands of the sea, than the number of those who hastened to pass. Where are they? Who can tell us? *Happy the dead who die in the Lord!*

Those who saw them, have told that great sadness was in their heart: agony heaved their chest, and as if fatigued by the labor of living, raising their eyes towards Heaven, they wept. Where are they? Who can tell us? *Happy the dead who die in the Lord!*

From the unknown places, where the river loses itself, two voices arise incessantly:

The one says: *From the depths I have cried unto Thee, O Lord: Lord hear my voice. Let Thy ears be attentive to the voice of my supplication. If thou wilt observe iniquities, O Lord: Lord, who shall endure it? But with the Lord there is mercy, and with Him plentiful redemption.*[1]

And the other: *We praise Thee, O God! We*

bless Thee: holy, holy, holy, is the Lord God of Hosts. Heaven and earth are full of Thy glory.[2]

And we also, we shall go there, whence proceed those lamentations or those songs of triumph. Where shall we be? Who can tell us? *Happy the dead who die in the Lord!*

---

(1) De profundis.
(2) Te Deum laudamus.

www.ingramcontent.com/pod-product-compliance
Lightning Source LLC
Chambersburg PA
CBHW020240170426
43202CB00008B/167